Angels
Friends in
High Places

Angels
Friends in
High Places

JERRY ORTHNER

CARMEL • NEW YORK 10512

This Guideposts edition is published by special arrangement with Christian Publications, Inc.

ISBN: 0-88965138-8
LOC Catalog Card Number:

© 1997 by Christian Publications, Inc.

Unless otherwise indicated,
Scripture taken from the HOLY BIBLE:
NEW INTERNATIONAL VERSION ®
© 1973, 1978, 1984 by the International Bible Society.
Used by permission of Zondervan Bible Publishers.

Jacket and design by José R. Fonfrias
Typeset by Composition Technologies, Inc.

To Karen
The wind beneath my wings

Your constant encouragement
and relentless affirmation
are the aerodynamics which keep this
husband, father and pastor
flying with the angels.

Contents

ACKNOWLEDGMENTS   xiii

INTRODUCTION   xv

CHAPTER 1
Angels: Identified Flying Objects   1

Are angels real? Can they be identified and described? Do we know anything about them for sure? Where did they come from? Take the lid off your brain as we go in search of the invisible inhabitants of our infinite universe.

CHAPTER 2
Friends in High Places Described   13

The Bible assumes the existence of angels and by observing their actions we can answer many of our questions about them. Like, just how many angels are there? What are they like (besides fast)? Do they really have wings? A sense of humor? What difference does any of this make in my life?

CHAPTER 3
Job Description of an Angel, Part I   32

Angels are all about us and they are very busy. They also have a very specific job description. So what does a day in the life of an angel look like anyway? What do they do? Anything for me?

CHAPTER 4

Job Description of an Angel, Part II   44

More amazing details on what angels do. The Bible is clear: God's people are guaranteed the ministry of angels in this present life and in the transition from this life to the next. If this information doesn't encourage you, nothing will.

CHAPTER 5

The Rise and Fall of a Beautiful Angel   58

Angelology (the study of angels) is really about the good, the bad and the ugly. No study of angels is complete without looking at the "bad and the ugly" too. So what about bad angels? Is the devil a fallen angel? Is there even a real devil? If so, where did he come from and where is he going? What is he like? What does he do? What has all this got to do with me?

CHAPTER 6

Job Description of a Fallen Angel   73

Like good angels, bad angels are very busy too. What does the day in the life of a fallen angel look like? What is it like to be a "wannabe" who will always be a "neverbe"?

CHAPTER 7

Old Angels in a New Age   80

What is the New Age? What do its followers believe? Why do they believe it? And what does the recent angel craze have to do with the spiritual renaissance that is sweeping our land?

CHAPTER 8

Entertaining Angels   *101*

You never know when you may be in the company of an angel. So, smile. Be kind to everyone you meet. Someday, somewhere, somehow, when you least expect it, you may entertain an angel unawares.

CHAPTER 9

Be an "Angel"!   *116*

The highest human calling is to be an agent of God's grace, a messenger of hope to a hurting world. The ultimate challenge is to be an "angel" yourself. Are you up to it? You may be the only "angel" someone will ever meet.

CHAPTER 10

Heaven, Harps, Halos and Clouds   *125*

What good is new, even fascinating information and knowledge unless you act on it, unless it produces some positive change in your life? The stories about God and His angels contain propositional truth. Your response to it can radically change your life and the way you live it today, tomorrow and for eternity.

APPENDICES: PERSONAL STORIES

Introduction to Personal Stories   *135*

APPENDIX 1

Angels Announcing and Forewarning

WARNING SIGNALS   Alone on the dark streets of an unfamiliar European city, Miriam Charter and her friend will never forget the mysterious stranger who directed them away from danger 137

APPENDIX 2

Angels Strengthening and Encouraging—Physically, Emotionally, Spiritually

AND THEN THE ANGEL CAME   Myrtle A. Hamm Robinson faced death from congenital heart disease until the angel came and gave her a new heart 140

YOHAN AND THE ANGEL   A special young man is strengthened and encouraged in an unusual and beautiful way 143

THE HOUSE CALL   Cecil M. Smith awakens one night to angelic "fingers" working his spinal column back into alignment 146

ADRIFT ON A CLOUD   Angels are sent to Anne M. Dick to help her through the most painful week in her life 147

ANGEL WATCHING OVER HER   Sandy Brown and her husband are encouraged by the heavenly confirmation of a life-changing decision 148

ANGEL AT THE BUS   Derek L. Hastings receives some surprising and unexpected affirmation from a stranger on a bus 150

PEACE ANGEL   Years after a harrowing experience, a young girl reveals why she wasn't frightened 152

THE "HALLELUJAH CHORUS" WITH EXTRA NOTES   A young boy needs something special to reassure him of God's love 153

APPENDIX 3

Angels Protecting and Defending

ANGEL VERSUS THE KHMER ROUGE A refugee camp in Thailand is
protected by unexplained soldiers 155

ANGELS AT RAMANGORD A pastor gets an unexpected illustration for his
Christmas message 159

ANGELS IN THE GULCH Long after the fact, a would-be assassin
describes the supernatural choir that thwarted his deadly intentions 161

ANGELS—A PART OF LIFE Oliver J. Abrams relates not one, but four
experiences that all point to the involvement of friends from high places
in his life 162

THE UNSEEN PROTECTOR How does a ninety-three-year-old woman fall
down a flight of sixteen stairs without injury or even bruises? 167

APPENDIX 4

Angels Delivering

ANGEL IN THE PASSENGER SEAT Rod Gammon receives some unexpected
emergency assistance for the ride of his life. 169

CLOSE CALL OVER OHIO Pilot David M. Fields and his passengers
benefit from life-saving radio warnings, which "didn't" happen, from an
air traffic controller who "didn't" exist 172

THE MAN IN THE OLD WHITE CAR Edward Nanno believes that on one
of the most fearful nights of his life an angel delivered him to his front
door. 174

A P P E N D I X 5

Angels and Prayer

SPECIAL DELIVERY   The amazing answer to the Dungans' prayers redefines
"special delivery.". 178

GUARDS IN WHITE!   For an imperiled daughter there's a surprising answer
to a mother's prayers from across the globe 179

DENNY   A mysterious yet honest stranger leaves no forwarding address,
only the misplaced valuable documents of a distraught and frantic
woman 181

LORD, HELP ME!   A traveler's cry for help is quietly met by a fleeting
Presence. 185

A P P E N D I X 6

Angels and the Dying

THE HOMEGOING   A mother dies and a young daughter is gently and
kindly comforted. 188

SONGS FOR A HEAVEN-SENT BOY   Explains the touching epitaph etched
on a tiny headstone: May God's angels always sing for Frederick Lumley
Chapman, May 18, 1964–September 17, 1967. 189

ENDNOTES   193

⁓ *Acknowledgments* ⁓

CHARLES LAMB SAID: "I love to lose myself in other people's minds. When I am not walking I am reading; I cannot sit and think. Books think for me."

I relate to that. And so too Solomon who correctly observed, "There is nothing new under the sun" (Ecclesiastes 1:9). Although the recent barrage of interest and the avalanche of information about angels would suggest otherwise, the same is true about them. Angels have been around for a long time and so has some fine thinking and writing on the topic.

To the many people whose books, tapes, essays and poems (some new, some old, some very old) did much of my thinking for me, I owe my sincere gratitude. But mostly to God for His quintessential angel resource, the Bible. It is by far the oldest, best, most comprehensive and reliable treatise on not only angels, but everything else that matters to human beings.

A book is a journey. Or perhaps in this case, a flight pattern. The takeoff for this one was a series of Christmas messages (1994) I presented to the most appreciative listeners a preacher could dream of. Hats off to the gracious and responsive congregation of Portage Alliance Church! Then, a special thanks to a long-time friend, Bill Goetz, who believing these ideas would fly as a book, helped launch it with his initial enthusiasm and affirmation. Once off the ground, I salute Marilynne Foster for keeping it airborne. Her expertise in editing and timely, personal encouragement kept it (and me!) from crashing many times. Fortunately, neither did, and now it lands safely in hands of you the reader. I hope it's a happy landing. Life is a journey too. Hopefully your reading this book will help to move you along in yours, as writing it has helped to move me along in mine.

Then to the numerous individuals who contributed to this book with their own personal, extraordinary experiences, what can I say? Thank you for letting us into your private world and giving us a glimpse of God's personal and special grace toward you. Your blessing has become ours and we are all drawn closer to God as a result.

To the staff (my friends and colleagues) of Portage Alliance Church who though I was coming in late and bedraggled for the last several months exclusively because of our newborn, when all along it was this "private" project, which was really robbing me of sleep—thank you for the gift of politely ignoring my truancy and blessing me in spite of it all. Your patient endurance and prayers did not go unnoticed.

Through this project I have not only been struck by how human angels are, but by how angelic humans can be. And so, finally, to my own little angelic squadron—my best friend, cherished confidante and faithful partner of eleven years, Karen; five-year-old daughter, Kate "Special Kathryn Gorgeous"; and infant, Sophia, the original "happy face"—you are loved! Although angels usually appear as males in Scripture, because of "my girls" I'll always wonder about that. God bless you each one. Your love, patience and understanding has and continues to be, in a word, "angelic."

And if earthlings *could* become heavenly angels, then surely my father would be one. To Dad. They just don't come any better.

Introduction

An Age of Angels Takes Flight

ON DECEMBER 27, 1993, a winged maiden in a gossamer gown perched gracefully on the cover of *Time* magazine. *"The New Age of Angels"* (cover title) was poised for flight. Inside, the feature article, "Angels Among Us," documented the surprising takeoff:

> *Suddenly the heavenly host is upon us, and in the New Age a grass roots revolution of the spirit in the U.S. has people asking all sorts of questions about angels.*

According to the *Time*/CNN poll, sixty-nine percent of people believed in the existence of angels. That was four years ago and "angelmania" shows no signs of landing. In fact, three years later, a "be-winged" and bare-chested Woody Harrelson hovers *on* (but doesn't do any favors *to*) the Christmas cover of *George* (December 1996). I have to say that *Time*'s choice of an 1889 original oil by Abbot Thayer is a tad more convincing than the gaunt thirty-five-year-old New Age seeker/actor of *Cheers* fame with wings strapped on his back and a George Washington tattoo affixed to his belly. In any case, the research within confirmed the still rising phenomenon—seventy-eight percent of Americans now believe in angels.

Angels are everywhere, still flying higher and further in public opinion and awareness like never before. Angels flutter on our calendars, coffee mugs and popcorn tins. Magazine covers, mail order catalogs and postage stamps. They flap in movies, talk shows and television specials. On CBS with Patty Duke. On PBS with Debra Winger. Prime time angels in *Touched by an Angel*. Re-run angels in *Highway to Heaven*. Angels chortling in popular music lyrics. An "Angel" record company. Acting angels on Broadway—*Angels in America*. Best-selling angels "sailing" out of New Age bookstores, Christian bookstores, comic-book bookstores. Angels in sports. Baseball's California Angels. Hockey's New Jersey Angels (albeit fallen ones, i.e., Devils). Angels, if you can believe it, in the outfield. And now, rings around Jupiter? Or are they halos? They *are* getting around.

You've noticed, haven't you? More and more the supernatural is permeating our lives. There is a huge spiritual renaissance percolating in our world, which is marked by an infatuation with the mystical, with the otherworldly, with angels. Is it mere curiosity that is motivating a generation of spiritual seekers? Partly.

But what I have discovered by studying and observing society's recent preoccupation and fascination with ethereal beings is that it is really just another expression of our relentless search for the sacred. I believe at the root of our search for angels is really a search for God. Let's face it. Life can be pretty brutal today. The global pains of war, hunger, AIDS, crime, drugs and violence are ever before us. The virulent hatred, epidemic loneliness and fear, and escalating evil on a pervasive scale have us desperately looking "out there," "up there," "anywhere," for hope, help, deliverance, salvation.

Well, is there anybody "out there"? The answer is, "yes." Angels? Yes. Human beings have potential *friends* in high places and they do fill the invisible realm around us. Is there anybody else? Yes, and even more important than they. Each of us also has a potential *friend* in high places, the Creator of both angels and earthlings, God. The Bible tells us a lot about both, but on one thing it is especially clear: how to connect with the Creator (God), not the created, i.e., angels. Therefore, if our search for angels leads us anywhere, it will properly lead us to God. If we connect with anyone in the process, let us connect with God.

This book, then, is not another "angel encounter" book, although dozens of amazing stories are contained in these pages. It is really a book about God and how to encounter Him. Its intention is not to wow you with the mysterious necessarily, but to wow you with God. Angel crazes and the like will come and go, but human emptiness without God in a life will always be there. Angelmania will eventually be replaced with some other phenomenon, which will merely be the next expression of our timeless search and longing within to know God. And what St. Augustine concluded (in his "Confessions") sixteen centuries ago will still be just as true: "Thou [God] hast made us for thyself, and restless is our heart until it come to rest in thee."

I hope that as a result of our look into the current flight of angels, your faith in God will take off too. And when you touch down on the final pages, may you be more at rest in Him. Not that the angels won't rejoice and take flight along with you. They will. But to know God first and enjoy Him forever, *that* is the chief end of us all. The ministry and assistance of angels which follows are merely a bonus—but what a bonus they are!

To that end and to His glory, then, bring 'em on. An age of angels has taken flight. Fasten your seat belts, tighten down your halos and come along for the flight. This book could change your life.

Jerry Orthner
January, 1997

Angels: Identified Flying Objects

T IS SAID THAT SOMETIMES late at night Theodore Roosevelt, the twenty-sixth president of the United States, and his friend, naturalist William Beebe, would go out and gaze at the clear night skies searching for a tiny patch of light near the constellation of Pegasus.

"This is the Spiral Galaxy in Andromeda," they would chant. "It is as large as our Milky Way. It is one of 100 million galaxies. It consists of 100 billion suns, each larger than our sun."

Then Teddy would turn to Willy and gasp, "Well, now I think we are small enough. Let's go to bed."

Have you ever turtled your head out of a sleeping bag and just watched nature's midnight IMAX™ unfold—the clear night sky freckled with glittering, stuttering stars suspended sparkling spillions of scattered miles away, and then, suddenly, felt really, really small? Lilliputian small? Cellular small? Insignificantly small?

You should. Because you are.

Your planet is huge. About 8,400 miles (12,713 kilometers) in diameter huge to be exact.

Feel small enough yet? No?

Look up!

The sun, 100 million miles (150 million kilometers) away from earth, checks in at about 920,000 miles (1,392,000 kilometers) in diameter, 109 times that of the earth! Keep looking (or imagining at this point). That sun is surrounded by stars. Billions of stars, some easily a thousand times larger (and hotter) than the sun! The nearest star to us is 4.3 light years away—26 trillion miles (40 trillion kilometers), give or take a million or two. No wonder all they do is twinkle!

The general theory of relativity describes the large-scale structure of just the observable universe alone on scales from one kilometer to a million million million million kilometers (one with twenty-four zeros after it).[1] We live in an infinite universe. Looking up into space, we gaze into endlessness. What's out there beside NASA™ litter? Have you ever wondered?

For the next several pages, let's wonder. Take the lid off your brain and let your imagination soar as we go in search of the invisible inhabitants of our infinite universe—extraterrestrials.

As in UFOs? Well, the majority of you reading this believe UFOs exist. A recent Angus Reid poll discovered that seven out of ten Canadians do and most believe that they are friendly. But are UFOs angels? Some think so. Many people contend that UFOs are part of God's invisible army presiding over the affairs of His creation—good angels. Others see a connection between UFOs and angels of the fallen variety intentionally materializing and appearing as extraterrestrials in order to be accepted, even welcomed by a generation desperately seeking hope.[2]

But are UFOs angels, friends and/or enemies in high places? No one knows for sure. But what we do know for sure is that there are IFOs (Identifiable Flying Objects) in the universe, saucer-shaped or not, and they are called angels. The Bible clearly reveals that celestial beings, quite distinct from God and from us, really do exist. And there are friendly ones and hostile ones. And they literally fill the invisible void around us, from the Milky Way to the tips of our noses. What's more, angels have mingled in the affairs of us terrestrials for centuries.

The angels keep their ancient places—
Turn but a stone and start a wing!
'Tis ye, 'tis ye, your estranged faces
That miss the many-splendored thing.

—Francis Thompson
(The Kingdom of God)

GUARDS, HUNDREDS OF THEM

There's an old book in my father's library that reads more like the adventures of Indiana Jones than a biography of a missionary to the New Hebrides.[3] It is, however, an authentic version of the latter.

We always need God. But sometimes we really need Him. Living under the constant threat of hostile natives gave John Paton several occasions to really need Him. It is often in our moments of peril or desperation that we "trip a stone and start a wing."

Confronting hostility was a part of everyday life for the Patons. But whether cornered on a jungle trail by a single cannibal warrior or surrounded by a host of them, miraculous deliverance also became a regular occurence.

One night, as far as the eye could see, the shore was covered with a dense host of frantic natives rushing the village. Paton and his people cried out to God for protection. Then, only 300 yards away, the host became suddenly still. An entire band of angry, frenzied, knife-wielding men, freeze-framed against the horizon. A tense and cadavorous silence followed as the villagers held their collective breaths and prayed "as one can only pray when in the jaws of death and on the brink of Eternity."

Then, without natural explanation, the entire band spun on their heels and disappeared into the bush by the harbor. "I know not why they turned," remembered Rev. Paton, "but I have no doubt it was the doing of God to save our lives."

Was it? Did God protect them with His angels? A subsequent event suggests that He did, not only there, but on several other occasions as well. A year later, following another almost identical foiled attack and retreat, the ambushing chief became a Christian. John Paton now had his chance to ask why they fled without explanation. The chief had a very good one: "Because of the hundreds of armed guards in shining armor circling your mission! Why else?" Paton insisted they were alone, but the chief knew what he saw.

What did he see? Did God answer the Patons' prayers by sending a squadron of protecting angels? It had happened before.

There's another old book (actually several) in my father's library that suggests He did. The Bible recounts a striking historic parallel in Second Kings 6:15–17. Elisha the prophet and his helper woke up one morning to an entire army closing in on them. Watch what happened:

> When the servant of the man of God [Elisha] got up and went out early the next morning, an army with horses and chariots had surrounded the city. "Oh, my lord, what shall we do?" the servant asked.
>
> "Don't be afraid," the prophet answered. "Those who are with us are more than those who are with them."
>
> And Elisha prayed, "O LORD, open his eyes so he may see." Then the LORD opened the servant's eyes, and he looked and saw the hills full of horses and chariots of fire all around Elisha.

But that's the Bible! That's the mission field! You expect supernatural events to occur in there and out there! But surely, not to me. Not here. Not now. Not today.
Oh?

> *The familiar scene is suddenly strange*
> *...the well known is what we have yet to learn,*
> *And two worlds meet, and intersect,*
> *and change.*
>
> —T.S. ELIOT
> *(To Walter de la Mare)*

THE WHITE CAVALRY

During the summer of 1918, heavy German shell fire had been directed against the battered town of Bethune, France. Would the Germans break through this strategic position and waltz on victoriously into Paris? It certainly looked that way.

An entire beleaguered British nation was called to emergency prayer. Almost in direct response, strangely, the enemy shell fire began to lift. Suddenly, a lark sprang up from a nearby meadow to announce what seemed to be the erratic and frightened retreat of the apparent victors.

What happened? The answer came from the mouth of a Prussian officer himself soon after his capture. British Staff Captain, Cecil Wightwick Haywood, was there to document the statement given by the senior officer.

The order had been given to advance in mass formation, and our troops were marching behind us singing their way to victory when Fritz, my lieutenant here, said: "Herr Kapitan, just look at that open ground behind Bethune, there is a Brigade of Cavalry coming up through the smoke drifting across it. They must be mad, these English, to advance against such a force as ours in the open. I suppose they must be Cavalry of one of their Colonial Forces, for see, they are all in white uniform and are mounted on white horses."

"Strange," I said, "I never heard of the English having any white uniformed cavalry, whether Colonial or not. They have all been fighting on foot for several years past, and anyway, they are in khaki, not white."

"Well, they are plain enough," he replied, "see, our guns have got their range now; they will be blown to pieces in no time."

We saw the shells bursting amongst the horses and their riders all of whom came forward at a quiet walk trot, in parade ground formation, each man and horse in his exact place.

Shortly afterward, our machine guns opened a heavy fire, raking the advance Cavalry with a dense hail of lead. But they came quietly forward, though the shells were bursting amongst them with intensified fury, and NOT A SINGLE MAN OR HORSE FELL.

Steadily they advanced, clear in the shining sunlight; and a few paces in front of them rode their Leader—a fine figure of a man, whose hair, like spun gold, shone in an aura round his bare head. By his side was a great sword, but his hands lay quietly holding his horse's reins, as his huge white charger bore him proudly forward.

In spite of heavy shell, and concentrated machine-gun fire, the White Cavalry advanced, remorseless as fate, like the incoming tide surging over a sandy beach.

Then a great FEAR fell on me, and I turned to flee; yes I, an Officer of the Prussian Guard, fled, panic-stricken, and around me were hundreds of terrified men, whimpering like children, throwing away their arms and accoutrements in order not to have their movements impeded…all running.

Their intense desire was to get away from that remorselessly advancing White Cavalry; but most of all from their awe-inspring Leader, whose hair shone like spun gold round his bare head, and whose hands lay quietly holding the reins of his great white charger.

That is all I have to tell you. We are beaten. The German Army is broken.

There may be fighting, but we have lost the War, we are beaten—by the White Cavalry...I cannot understand—I cannot understand...."[4]

But the people who prayed understood. They must have known that "the angel of the LORD encamps around those who fear him, and he delivers them. Taste and see that the LORD is good; blessed is the man who takes refuge in him." David journaled that in Psalm 34:7–8 in 930-something B.C. Could an ancient principle like this still hold true for us today? Did God answer the prayers of the British people and deliver them too? Could he do the same for you?

FACT: Human beings have potential friends in high places called holy angels. No doubt about it. They existed then. They exist now. And they are committed to constant service to God and, in turn, to His people. If that doesn't excite you, nothing will. The reality of angels is one of the most exciting, consistent, dependable truths in the whole Bible.

ANGELS, ANGELS, EVERYWHERE

Millions of spiritual creatures walk the earth
unseen, both when we wake and when we sleep.

—JOHN MILTON
(Paradise Lost, 1667)

And Milton's right. Psalm 68:17 tells us that the chariots of God are tens of thousands and thousands of thousands ("chariots of God" is a metaphor for angelic hosts, and "tens of thousands" is a metaphor for, let's see, probably a couple billion!). Myriads of angels—a ubiquitous, invisible mingling and bustling of them in a celestial dimension that we, in even our wildest dreams, can only imagine. So let's.

Put this book down for a minute. Look around your room (or if you're lucky enough to be outside, the sky). Your room, that sky, is full of angels, some holy ones and some not so holy ones. But there are angels all about us—all the time.

So what's the story? What do we know about them? Can we confidently know anything about them for sure? Gallons of ink have been spilled recently in an almost global barrage of material on angels. But is it reliable? Or is it merely speculative, tantalizing or sensational in nature? On what kind of truth source is it based?

ONE TRUTH SOURCE

Let me say it upfront and clearly: *Angels: Friends in High Places* uses a single identifiable truth source, a book that (speaking of ink) has had more gallons spilled printing its pages than even angel books. This totally reliable source is the Bible, which, incidentally, has held the whole truth and nothing but the truth for centuries; a book I believe (along with millions of others, based on the ink factor alone) contains a complete and comprehensive record of all we need to know about God and ultimate truth—including the truth about angels.

But if you pick up the latest book on angels from your local mall you will likely find precious few references to Scripture. What you will no doubt discover is a whole lot of fanciful guesswork and imaginative speculation. Unfortunately, if you begin with a philosophical opinion about angels, then the sky and your imagination is the limit, leaving you basically stuck "up in the air." But if you start with and maintain a biblical basis, then ultimate truth defines the limits and provides a solid grounding for belief and discussion.

> *Philosophy will clip an angel's wings.*
> —JOHN KEATS (1795–1821)

Sophie Burnham, considered a foremost angel authority, makes this stunning admission in her recent bestselling *Book of Angels:* "Look: we know nothing about angels. We do not know what angels are.... We know nothing of this other realm, except that we are given brief, fleeting glimpses in our hearts."[5] Apparently these mere glimpses are enough, for she promptly proceeds to write almost 300 pages about a topic she apparently knows "nothing" about. Interesting!

We can know a lot about angels. Angels literally punctuate the Scriptures. "Open the pages of Scripture and there's the rustle of angels," says Marilyn Carlson Webber.[6] Angels are everywhere, teaching us about themselves as we study and observe the over 270 references to them from Genesis to Revelation. In fact, it is safe to say that a Bible without angels is simply not a Bible. If you were to take all of the references to angels out of the Old Testament (108 of them), for example, it would look like Swiss cheese. Stories wouldn't make sense. Mysterious events couldn't be explained. Angels are everywhere in the Old Testament.

And what about the 165 or so references in the New Testament? Take the angels out of there and you might as well jettison the whole thing. Without angels, says John MacArthur, "the book of Revelation would be reduced to chapter headings since angels appear on virtually every page."[7] From cover to cover, the Bible literally rustles with the presence of angels.

Scripture assumes and affirms the existence of angels. Not only that, but their existence is also confirmed by the personal experiences of many of us (maybe even you, and certainly by those whose accounts appear in these pages) who have encountered angels in one form or another in their daily lives.

So, if they exist, where did they come from?

Where Did Angels Come From?

When we look at Jesus we see "God's original purpose in everything created. For everything, absolutely everything, above and below, visible and invisible, rank after rank after rank of angels—*everything* got started [was created] in him and finds its purpose in him" (Colossians 1:16–17, *The Message*).

Angels are create-ures (creatures). They were created. So are we. God created invisible creatures and visible creatures, heavenly creatures and earthly creatures, angels and earthlings!

> *Two things Thou has made,*
> *O Lord, one near to Thee—*
> *namely angelic substance,*
> *the other near to nothing—*
> *namely matter."*
>
> —AUGUSTINE

Perhaps you've never thought about it before, but there were "two" creations. The earth and all you see and the heavens and all you don't see.

Which came first? The angel or the earthling? I'm not sure Job was asking the same question, but in an energetic exchange with God recorded in Job 38, we inadvertently get our answer:

> Where were you [Job] when I laid the
> earth's foundation?
> Tell me, if you understand.
> Who marked off its dimensions?
> Surely you know!
> Who stretched a measuring line across it?
> On what were its footings set,
> or who laid its cornerstone—
> while the morning stars [another metaphor
> for angels] sang together
> and all the angels shouted for joy?
>
> (38:4–7)

Paraphrase: "Job, not you or anybody else was around when I created the earth. Only the angels were." So it seems that angels were created sometime before human beings and the material universe. How much before is a mystery, but we know that angels preceded earthlings because one of them (albeit a fallen one) is already slinking around the Garden of Eden when Adam and Eve finally come on the scene (Genesis 3:1).

No Mommy or Daddy Angels

Something else we know is that angels do not procreate. They were produced, but they do not reproduce. As many as there are today is as many as there ever will be. There are, therefore, no mommy angels or daddy angels. And, as my wife informed me when I came home for lunch the other day, there is no such thing as a four-year-old angel either!

No baby angels? Sorry, Rafaello (Renaissance master whose child angel graces a 1996 U.S. postage stamp). No bare-rumped, dimple-chinned, rosy-cheeked cherubs blowing fanfares on golden trumpets or shooting pointed arrows through young lovers' hearts? Cute thought, but just a thought.

St. Augustine thought angels "breed like flies" because there were so many. But Augustine was wrong (I've always wanted to say that). Angels don't breed. They were all directly, instantaneously and individually, yet simultaneously created by God with no capacity or wherewithal to reproduce.

They are not male (although they most often materialize as males in Scripture at least). They are not female. They are...angels, and as such, there are no Mr. and Mrs. Angel either. They do not marry. They have no need to marry. Only earthlings marry. And although this may come as a disappointment to some of you (and a relief to the rest), neither will human beings be married when we leave this earth.

Jesus, discussing this issue with some wishful thinkers in Matthew 22:30, put it this way (*The Message*): "You're off base.... You don't know your Bibles, and you don't know how God works. At the resurrection [i.e. in heaven] we're beyond marriage. As with the angels, all our ecstasies and intimacies then will be with God."

You see, our afterlife (where the angels already are) is a wholly new kind of existence in a completely different dimension, which is not simply a cosmic adaptation or modified version of what we already know and presently experience. It is a completely new and everlasting spiritual life where there is no need for marriage because the essential elements of marriage (procreation, cohabitation, interdependence, ecstasy and intimacy) are unnecessary. Our focus and attention will not be on each other (or angels for that matter) but on our Creator. Without a doubt, God alone will receive our riveted, awe-inspired attention for eons to come. God alone will be our singular heartthrob.

RECAP: Once upon a time, God created angels. Millions of them all at once. En masse. They do not, will not, cannot multiply. Neither do they grow old and die. They never have to worry about feathers falling out or receding halos. Their number is fixed and they do not change. Well, almost. Some did, once, but only once. It came when one of them (Lucifer, "Son of the Morning") flicked his "tail [and] knocked a third of the Stars [angels] from the sky and dumped them on earth" (Revelation 12:4, *The Message*). But each individual angel (fallen or holy) was created immortal and will exist forever, somewhere. Just like us. Some eternally separated from God. Some forever united with God. Just like us.

Friends in High Places Described

*Outside the open window the morning
is all awash with angels.*

—RICHARD PURDY WILBUR (1921–)

DID MUCH OF MY RESEARCH about angels alone at the lake one summer. Here's the scene. My computer is set up in a large screened-in deck overlooking a lawn and a beautiful lake. It's isolated, private, quiet—the perfect ingredients for serendipitous, spine-shivering reflections on supernatural themes.

One of them came early one morning while I was musing on the characteristic uniqueness of angels. I journaled the moment:

> Lift your eyes and look to the heavens:
>   Who created all these?
> He who brings out the starry host
>   one by one,
> and calls them *each by name*.
> (Isaiah 40:26)

It's morning. Deathly calm, idle, motionless. A thick, heavy quilt of dense fog is suspended over the lake, lawn and cottage. It feels like it is going to drop any moment and swallow me up into a netherworld. And yet, there is an awkward sense of the peaceful and heavenly in the surrealism of it all.

Looking up from my desk, I notice the subtle movement of the lawn as if it were alive. Closer inspection reveals four ashen seagulls strutting through the fog. Like animated porcelain lawn ornaments, they glide…carefree… meandering softly about the wet grass. I watch them for several minutes.

I've never really looked at a seagull before. I've "seen" plenty of seagulls. Never "looked" at one. I've always thought of them as roadkill scavengers with french fries or dead gopher parts in their beaks. But these birds…these gulls are beautiful. I think I could learn to appreciate them for the first time in my life.

I am reminded of Samuel Taylor Coleridge's *Rime of the Ancient Mariner* (1798). That beautiful, redemptive, liberating moment where the cynical, cursed old sailor finally recognizes the beauty in the common, ordinary, unattractive, even ugly creatures of the sea. With admiration replacing disdain, he cries:

> O happy living things! No tongue
> Their beauty might declare.
> A spring of love gushed from my heart
> And I blessed them unaware;
> Sure my kind saint took pity on me
> And I blessed them unaware.

Four beautiful seagulls. All recognizably seagulls, but each so completely different. One gray with white spots. One mostly gray. One just gray. One just plain, solid white.

That's it! The eerie similarity rattles a chill down my backbone. Angels, too, are uniquely different. Like seagulls. Like snowflakes. Like us! Independently crafted and singularly valuable. What an amazing Creator of us all!

You alone are the LORD. You made the heavens, even the highest heavens, and all their starry host, the earth and all that is on it, the seas and all that is in them. You give life to everything, and the multitudes of heaven worship you. (Nehemiah 9:6)

HOW MANY ANGELS ARE THERE?

More than four. The Bible doesn't tell us exactly, but it does give some graphic estimates: "Then I [John] looked and heard the voice of many angels numbering thousands upon thousands, and ten thousand times ten thousand. They encircled the throne and the living creatures and the elders" (Revelation 5:11).

Let's just say there were a few hundred million in this little ensemble alone. But Hebrews 12:22 stops the guessing: "But you have come to Mount Zion and to the city of the living God, the heavenly Jerusalem, to an *innumerable company of angels*" (emphasis mine, NKJV). This verse's allusion to an even approximate angel count is one of the great superlatives of Scripture. The New American Standard Version says, "myriads!" *The Message*, "throngs." The NIV, "thousands upon thousands."

How many angels exist? Literal answer: "Don't even try to figure it out. You can't count that high!" Now are you beginning to get a sense of why the universe is so infinitely vast—to house its infinite number of occupants?! Occupants who at one time or another can be seen gathered *en masse* in a festive crescendo of praise and worship to God (Hebrews 12:22, Revelation 4–5). Heavenly beings, who at other times, may be sweeping about the universe to carry out a command of God. Sometimes they fly solo; sometimes in organized squadrons. Sometimes as only one of an entire invisible army, they come flashing to the rescue of God's people, swords brandished and flags waving (2 Kings 19:14–36).

Sometimes we find them wrestling with enemy angels or racing on "prayer-answering detail" to a fellow angel's rescue (Daniel 10:12–14) or to ours. Often they are seen trafficking about our planet, mingling in the affairs of its inhabitants by delivering, protecting, forewarning or quietly comforting and encouraging (1 Kings 19:5; Luke 22:43). Yes, they are out there. They are right here. They are busy. And they are many.

They are Gabriel, "the hero of God," "the messenger of God" (Luke 1:19, 26), "the mighty one." Michael the archangel ("who is like God?") (Jude 9), "the great prince" (Daniel 12:1; 10:21). Seraphim, the "burners" or "fiery ones" (Isaiah 6:1–3). Cherubim, the covering "guards" (Genesis 3:24) and "protectors." Thrones, dominions, principalities, authorities and powers (Ephesians 6:12). Holy ones (Psalm 89:5). Elect ones (1 Timothy 5:21). Sons of the Mighty (Psalm 89:6). Sons of God (Job 1:6, 2:1, 38:7). Heavenly beings (Psalm 89:6). Starry hosts (Isaiah 40:26). Morning stars (Job 38:7). All of these and more. Billions more. And all of them created in a mini-micro-nano second as God literally thought them into existence!

How many angels are there? Maybe this is the best answer: One, who affects your life, is plenty.

WHAT ARE ANGELS LIKE (BESIDES FAST)?

Scripture clearly presents angels as personal creatures, not the ethereal, winged maidens of medieval or Renaissance art hovering gracefully over pensive nativity scenes. Neither are angels mechanical, serial-numbered cosmic robots programed for windup search and rescue (or destroy) missions. They are personal beings who possess all the traits of personality that you and I have: intelligence, will and emotions. They are so personal they even have their own names (Isaiah 40:26).

Angels Are Intelligent

Ezekiel 28:12 describes one of them, Lucifer, in his original state—as a "model of perfection, full of wisdom and perfect in beauty." Later, in his fallen state, this same angel uses his intelligence to skillfully, but unsuccessfully test Jesus (Luke 4).

In chapter 9 of the Old Testament book that bears his name, Daniel describes how an angel came to him "in swift flight about the time of the evening sacrifice. He instructed me and said to me, 'Daniel, I have now come to give you insight and understanding'" (9:21–22). This angel (Gabriel, as it turns out) somehow understood Daniel's prayer, was dispatched and sped quickly in response to it, then provided insight and understanding based on it. He was intelligent and therefore able to inform, guide, direct and communicate wisdom and understanding.

Yes, angels are astute, even brilliant (2 Samuel 14:20), but they don't know everything. Only God is omniscient (all-knowing). For example, it might surprise you that not even angels fully comprehend the mystery of God's message of salvation for human beings. In the first century, the apostle Peter wrote a letter to encourage some human friends. "What a God we have!" he wrote in First Peter 1:2, "And how fortunate we are to have him, this Father of our Master Jesus! Because Jesus was raised from the dead, we've been given a brand-new life and have everything to live for, including a future in heaven— and the future starts now!" *(The Message)*.

Peter goes on to develop these life-giving thoughts a bit and then, in verse 12, he slips in a very intriguing revelation, that if you are reading fast you might well miss. Reminding them again of how important it is for human beings to not only understand, but personalize and embellish this message, Peter says: "Do you realize how fortunate you are? Angels would have given anything to be in on this!"

Isn't that interesting! Salvation is for men and women exclusively. Never having sinned, angels do not need, let alone comprehend, a need for redemption. They are up there scratching their halos trying to figure out why God would go to such extreme lengths to rescue human beings from eternal punishment. It is a mystery to them why (take a deep breath) God would voluntarily make Himself lower than the angels themselves (Hebrews 2:9) to take on the form of a human being of all things, temporarily self-imposing massive limitations upon His divine attributes; exit infinity; enter the finite; humbly intersect historical time and space; boldly live a perfect, sinless life on earth, then allow Himself to be misunderstood and violently tortured for His efforts, yet in so doing, voluntarily bear the sins of an undeserving and largely ungrateful world on His own shoulders (Philippians 2:5–11). Then die, taking our sins with Him to the grave, unload them, rise from the dead and return to circulation as a man again, having conquered death, so that whoever would believe He did all this for them and would respond by following Him would not be destroyed, but could have a whole and everlasting life (John 3:16).

Whew! Come to think of it, that doesn't make a whole lot of sense to me either, but I like the sound of it. And if you are a seeker of spiritual truth and you haven't figured out the message of Christianity yet (sounds too confusing to believe or too good to be true), you're in good company—angels. Keep searching. You may very well one day gain one up on the angels on this one. In fact, if you are diligent and sincere, God promises that you will eventually find Him (Matthew 7:7). To every seeking person comes a revealing God. Keep seeking. You will understand one day.

It should be noted that there is one group of beings who do fully comprehend salvation, but it doesn't do them any good. Fallen angels will never get it. Unlike holy angels who have never sinned and therefore have no need of redemption, fallen angels have sinned, but they have no hope of redemption.

You see, the fate of all angels is sealed forever. Holy angels will spend eternity with God, fallen angels separated from God. When some of them fell to earth, the fall was final, forever and irreversible. Their eternal residence is already prepared and their reservations are confirmed. It is only a matter of time before they are separated from God and His angels and His people forever (Revelation 20). Until then, their only *raison d'etre*, their singular agenda, is to convince or deceive men and women toward a similar fate. That's it. Basically, that's all they do, all day long.

Listen, God offers you so much more than they will ever have. "For God so loved the world that he gave his one and only Son, that whoever believes in him shall not perish but have eternal life" (John 3:16). As the apostle Peter might add, "Do you realize how fortunate you are to have read this?"

> *The angels are His messengers; we His sheep.*
> *He set their table in heaven; He filled our manger*
> *on earth. So that man might eat the bread*
> *of angels, the Creator of angels became man.*
> *The angels praise Him by living, we by believing;*
> *they by enjoying, we by seeking; they by*
> *entering, we by knocking.*
>
> —ADAPTED FROM *SERMONS ON THE*
> *LITURGICAL SEASON* BY ST. AUGUSTINE

Angels Have a Will

Another personality trait demonstrated by angels is the capacity for self-determination or will. They have the ability to choose, make decisions and follow through on them. In the New Testament book of Hebrews, for example, God appeals to their wills. "Let all God's angels worship him [Jesus]" (Hebrews 1:6). This invitation seems to indicate the capacity to choose and begs an appropriate response or exercise of the will from the hearer(s). Indeed, the capacity for self-determination is what got them in trouble the one time some did. Five times, Isaiah 14 informs us, Lucifer dug his heels in and "I willed" himself right out of God's heaven along with one-third of the rest of the angels who emphatically "me too'd" right along with him. Yes, angels have a will too. Some choose to do good; others evil.

Angels Have Emotions

Good night, sweet prince:
and flights of angels
sing thee to thy rest."

—WILLIAM SHAKESPEARE
(Hamlet)

Singing, worshiping, celebrating and cheering involves emotional expressions of joy. Angels do all of the above. Job 38:7 says the angels sang together at creation. A festive throng surrounds the throne in Hebrews 12:22. "Thousands upon thousands, and ten thousand times ten thousand" are in full song at the end of time in Revelation 5:11. Angels can sing. What's more, they love to sing.

First Corinthians 13:1 suggests there is a language of men and a language of angels. If you can't sing, this may be good news for you. In his book *Angels: God's Secret Agents*, Billy Graham, who admittedly can't carry a tune, yearns for the celestial music lessons he believes are forthcoming for believers in heaven.[1] I hope he's right.

Speaking of believers, were you aware that every time a human being chooses to follow Jesus Christ instead of Wycliffe (the Bible calls this repentance), the angels celebrate? Luke illustrates this truth with the story of a woman who threw a block party after she rediscovered a valuable possession. "Celebrate with me!" she announces to her friends and neighbors in Luke 15:9. "I found my lost coin!" Luke adds, "Count on it—that's the kind of party God's angels throw every time one lost soul turns to God" (15:10, *The Message*).

Imagine the "Hip! Hip! Hooray!" of a zillion or so of God's finest for little old you! Did you ever stop to think you are that valuable to God? Has anybody ever cheered for you for anything? Did you ever stop to think you might mean that much to anybody? You do. Think on it. Myriads (millions) of angels, busy as they are, literally stopping in their tracks and whooping it up over you...just you! Maybe you don't have a very high opinion of yourself. Maybe you feel unloved or unloving. Maybe you cannot or never will perceive your intrinsic value from where you sit today, but in the spiritual dimension, in the eternal sphere and scheme of things, you, my friend, are incredibly treasured by God and His angels. The best friends you could ever have are the ones in high places.

Angels are always looking for an excuse to celebrate, and when they are not celebrating your spiritual landmarks, they are celebrating God's. Angels are predominantly worshiping creatures. They loudly and unabashedly express deep and sincere emotions of reverence, awe, honor and glory to their Creator (Revelation 5:11–12; 7:11–12). When they are not busying themselves in ministry to God, they are worshiping Him. They love God like some of you and simply cannot restrain themselves in His presence, like some of you. When you stop and think about it, angels are a lot like us. And yet, we differ.

ANGELS AND EARTHLINGS: SIMILARITIES AND DIFFERENCES

For man is joined spirit and body...visible
and invisible, two worlds meet in man."

—T.S. ELIOT
("Choruses from the Rock IX")

Earthlings have a visible and an invisible component. Angels are all "invisible" (Colossians 1:16). They are non-material, although they can and do materialize for special missions in the material world.

Humans are spirit (or soul) plus flesh plus blood. Angels are spirit, period, a person without the flesh and the blood (Luke 24:37–39). Angels do, however, have a body of sorts. First Corinthians 15:44 tells us there is a natural (physical) body and a spiritual (heavenly) body. An angel has the latter, a celestial body. And, as such, an angel has some kind of localized capacity, is restricted by spatial limitations and can be in only one place at a time.

Does being a spirit make an angel a god? Or God? Or Godlike? Not even close. Although God is also spirit, He alone is the all-present Spirit. Only God is everywhere saturating infinity. Angelic spirits fill only the void around them, restricted to one spot at a time. God never has to move anywhere. He is already here. There. Everywhere. Angels are not. But they can get from here to there quickly. Very quickly. Read Daniel 9 and 10.

So how can an angel, a spirit, be a person with the absence of a body? Isn't a person by definition a human being? Think. Is your body your personality? No, your personality, the expressive essence that defines your uniqueness, resides some-where within your body, namely, your spirit. That spirit (or soul), which occupies no space at all, believe it or not, is the real you, what makes you a person.

Your physical body occupies only a few cubic centimeters of space itself. It serves as a fragile life-support system for about seven or eight decades and is then discarded. Your spirit, on the other hand, occupies no well-defined space at all, but ironically, it *never* wears out. It is immortal. The body will age and decay, but the sense that I exist, the self-awareness of who I am in spirit remains eternally absolute and self-existent against all other fields of change. You (the real you) will continue to exist somewhere forever (Ecclesiastes 3:11), just like the angels. (Revelation 20:10)

DO ANGELS HAVE WINGS?

Angels from the realms of glory, wing their
flight o'er all the earth.

—JAMES MONTGOMERY (1771–1854)

According to every Christmas card, oil painting and doodle sketch known to bored students, angels have two wings. Outside the halo, harp and cloud, wings are the most distinguishing mark of an angel. The prophet Daniel saw one fly swiftly to him (Daniel 9:21). And it is true that the seraphim and cherubim are described as having wings. But that's not all they had. The cherubim in Ezekiel 10 also had hands, a torso of "whirling wheels," four faces and a montage of eyeballs covering the whole works. And then the wings, of course.

The seraphim in Isaiah 6:2 had six of them—two to cover their faces, two to cover their feet, and two with which to "fly," although one would worry about where, with their eyes covered and all! The bottom line is that angels are basically indescribable and the wings thing, if anything, is to suggest swiftness in response to God's commands. Wings, of course, are metaphors for speed, versatility and flight. And since the only creatures we know that can fly use wings, we picture or envision angels with similar apparatus.

So, we don't know if angels "wing their flight o'er all the earth" or not. But we do know that they "fly" swiftly in response to the summons of God. In their own dimension, they are incredibly fast!

DO ANGELS HAVE A SENSE OF HUMOR?

*Angels can fly because they
take themselves lightly.*
—G.K. CHESTERTON

Angels have a sense of humor. Why not? It's an important emotion. The book of Ecclesiastes identifies laughter as one of the necessary rhythms of life. A meaningful, abundant life will include laughter as well as tears. The Bible itself laughs. It is full of humorous situations and figures of speech. Many of its characters, like Abraham, Elijah and David laughed uproariously. Jesus Himself had a very keen wit and sense of humor using puns, irony, paradox, exaggeration, story and familiar anecdotes. If God laughs and people laugh, there is good reason to believe that the "other" creation (angels) take themselves lightly as well. Let me illustrate.

At least three elements are necessary for humor to be humor. One element is self-awareness, the ability to step back and see ourselves as creatures who have been wired up to express emotions. A second key element is the wherewithal not to take ourselves too seriously, to laugh at ourselves. Finally, for humor to exist there must be a contrast between the ideal and the real, the expected and the unexpected.[2] The essence of good humor is discrepancy, apparent contradiction, paradox…like pregnant ninety-year-olds and talking mules!

THREE MEN AND A BABY (*Genesis 18:1–15*)

It's 100 degrees in the shade of the old tent flap under which Abraham, whose age matches the temperature, is a breath away from a deep sleep. His vision is blurring. The landscape is growing hazy. Then suddenly, through the narrowing slits of his listing eyelids, three strangers materialize as if out of nowhere. "A mirage? Am I seeing things?"

It's ninety degrees in the tent in which Sarah (Abe's wife), whose age matches the temperature inside, is a breath away from her own dreamland. Suddenly, her old ears awaken to an apparent commotion from the vicinity where her husband is supposed to be asleep. "A dream? Am I hearing things?"

"No, Honey! We have guests. Quick! Three *seahs* of our best flour! Knead it and make some rolls!" (Probable reaction: "From scratch? You can't be serious!")

But Abraham, who is deadly serious, runs from the tent to his corral and rustles up the camp cook, whose reaction is not dissimilar to Sarah's: "Veal cutlets from scratch? Fresh yogurt? Who's coming to dinner?"

Four hours later Abraham, in an impressive display of spontaneous hospitality, presents a fine three-course meal to three total strangers under the shade of the old oak trees lining his campground. Sarah, meanwhile, takes up her strategic post to observe (hopefully unnoticed) the curious proceedings of this most unnatural event.

All her life Sarah had really wanted only one thing—a baby. And, in her prime, she tried everything available in her day, to no avail. Years of anticipation gradually hardened to resignation. Safe to say, at ninety, Sarah was no longer expectant, let alone expecting. It hardly even entered her mind anymore. Still...

"Abraham, where's your wife, Sarah?"

"My wife?" *How'd they know I have a wife named Sarah?* "In the tent. Why?"

"Oh, we are going to be back around these parts in about nine months or so and thought since you've been so kind to us and all, we'd like to bring a few gifts to her baby shower to show our appreciation."

Sarah, evesdropping, loses it. Four heads turn in tennis-match unison to the tent flap where Abraham's wife is laughing sarcastically. Then suddenly, embarrassed at her own feeble attempt at deception, she pulls her head back into the safety of her shell and listens nonplused to the same proclamation from the three strangers. This time she's not laughing.

"What's Sarah laughing at? Does she think she's too old to have a baby? Listen, Abraham, is anything too difficult for God? We'll be back in nine months for the shower. Count on it!"

With that the three strangers turn to leave. Sarah pokes her head once again from the tent flap, and with eyes still watery and complexion still flushed, shouts defensively, "I wasn't laughing!"

One stops in mid-stride, turns, and with a twinkle in his eye says, "Oh, yes you were."

Sarah turns, and with a finger to her chin thinks, *Who were they? How did they know it was me laughing? How did they know my name? Hmm, if they knew...then maybe...nah, couldn't be.*

Nine months later, a baby's cry and Sarah's laughter are vibrating the walls of father Abraham's tent. The angels got the last laugh, but Sarah's and Abe's joy has just begun. Taking the baby books down from the shelf they excitedly look up all the names under "laughter" and settle on Isaac (Genesis 21:3), "because," Sarah muses admiringly to the 101-year-old daddy, "God has brought me laughter, and everyone who hears about this will laugh with me" (Genesis 21:6). And so we do, Sarah.

God has a sense of humor. People have a sense of humor. And angels are in on it too. Postscript: Can't you just see Isaac in a few years taking his antique parents to school for "show and tell"?

One more story from the Bible (Numbers 22).

BALAAM AND MRS. ED

Here comes Balaam riding on his donkey. An angel has just been sent out by God to engender a little respect into the heart of this Hebrew prophet who is about to compromise his integrity by accepting a bribe from an enemy (King Balak) to curse Israel. The angel positions himself in the middle of the road with his sword drawn and pointed toward Balaam's heart. The donkey sees the angel. Balaam doesn't.

To save his master's life, the donkey hits the ditch. Balaam, nonplused, beats the donkey back up onto the road. The angel is still there, poised to pierce. Again, the donkey sees the angel. Again, Balaam doesn't. You guessed it. The donkey leans to the right to dodge the weapon, thereby crushing his master's foot against a brick wall. He receives another beating for his efforts and seriously begins to wonder if saving his master's life is worth the effort.

Scripture goes on to recount: "Then the angel of the LORD moved on ahead and stood in a narrow place where there was no room to turn, either to the right or to the left. When the donkey saw the angel of the LORD., she lay down under Balaam" (22:26–27). Boom! She drops on all fours! And Balaam was angry and, you guessed it, beats the donkey with his staff. "Then the LORD opened the donkey's mouth." And Mrs. Ed says to Balaam, "What have I done to you to make you beat me these three times?" (22:28).

Now, if you think a pet talking to its master is weird, picture this. "Balaam answered the donkey, 'You have made a fool of me! If I had a sword in my hand, I would kill you right now.' [Who am I talking to?!] The donkey said to Balaam, 'Am I not your own donkey, which you have always ridden, to this day? Have I been in the habit of doing this to you?'" (22:29–30).

"Well, come to think of it, no."

"Then the LORD opened Balaam's eyes, and he saw the angel of the LORD standing in the road with his sword drawn. So he bowed low and fell facedown" (22:31).

As it turns out, instead of accepting Balak's bribe and cursing Israel, Balaam obeys the Lord and blesses Israel. It took an unusual angelic encounter to convince Balaam that God wields a sword and disobedience can be deadly. This is a serious lesson of trust and obedience for us all, and a very funny story.

Angels communicate. Remember? Can you imagine that angel relating this story to his friends at the next day's debriefing? Or do you think that later that night Baalam would be able to recount the incident without cracking up? Or that 6,000 years down the road we would? Or what do you think happened when Mrs. Ed got back to the barn that night?

THREE WOMEN AND A BLOND

One more story—from the life and experience of one of my colleagues named Valerie.

Three single, non-French-speaking girls are crossing two West African countries. Does it sound like an opportunity for disaster? Well, it turned out to be a chance to see God's protection at work and a firsthand encounter with an angel.

"After a week of vacation with some Malian missionaries," Val says, "I caught a ride back to Ivory Coast with two other teachers at the missionary kids' (MK) school. We began our journey by filling up with gas and then immediately proceeded to take a wrong turn out of town. Unknown to us, we cheerfully drove for two hours in the opposite direction of our intended destination. We began to worry as the road became narrower and rougher, the towns less commercialized and the people less westernized. By now we were travelling aimlessly in unfamiliar, dense and potentially dangerous bush area.

"Beginning to worry about the gas situation and the few hours we had left before nightfall, we came upon a small village. There on the side of the road was a blond, curly-haired girl—a white girl—standing by a bush. We decided to stop and see if she needed any help, not realizing it was us who needed help!

" 'No,' she replied in perfect English. She didn't need any help, but she wondered aloud who we were and just where we thought we were going. Her exact reply to our response, all the while chewing gum and blowing bubbles, was, 'I've never heard of Ferkessedougou, but you are getting very close to the Senegal border!' She suggested we were going the wrong way (confirming our suspicions!) and should turn around, as there were no 'real' towns in the direction we were heading.

"We gratefully waved goodbye and sped (no speed limits in the African bush!) back in the direction from whence we came, retracing our tracks safely to the same gas station that launched our wayward journey.

"Later, safely tucked in bed in a guest house, I wondered about the girl we had met—muscular build, lots of blond curls, big army boots, chewing gum and all smiles. I couldn't (still can't) understand why she'd be where she was and where she got her bubble gum! It just didn't fit! I believe she was an angel sent by God to protect us from the very real dangers of an African border crossing or running out of gas at night. God even had a sense of humor to have her speak with a Southern drawl! When I remember her smile, I think of God smiling too."

Are angels above rescuing some vulnerable young women and cleverly tempering their fear with a few bubbles, some curls and a smile? Or are they just involved in big things, like riding white stallions and fending off attacking cannibals?

Matthew 18:10. Jesus is speaking to his disciples: "Watch it that you don't treat a single one of these childlike believers arrogantly. You realize, don't you, that their personal angels are constantly in touch with my Father in heaven?" (*The Message*).

Isn't that encouraging? Each one of God's children has at least one (perhaps more) angel assigned to him or her. And they are in constant contact with Him with your best interests in mind. Followers of Jesus (Christians) are in the very capable hands of some very special friends in high places—God and His angelic messengers.

So What?

Very intriguing creatures, these angels. And you may be saying, "This is interesting information, but so what?" Let me give you two "so what's." I see at least two implicit life-changing truths emerge from the first two chapters: (1) we have potential friends in high places called holy angels. No doubt about it. Angels exist and they are committed to constant service to God and in turn,

God's people. And (2) flowing out of this and underscoring everything you've read so far is something even more amazing: Each one of us has a potential Friend in high places (actually, all over the places) called God. We live in an infinite universe and when we look out into space, we look out into endlessness and we feel small and insignificant. But we are not so small that a big God is not interested in the smallest of us and the seemingly minute details of our existence. The same God who created heavenly messengers and knows and calls each by name knows and calls each of us by name. The Bible indicates that if your spiritual eyes were somehow opened, you wouldn't see a cosmic bully poised with a divine hammer (like some imagine) or even a distant or disinterested deity with His back turned to you. What you would see is the loving God of a limitless universe, with His arms outstretched, surrounded by a cast of admiring angels, calling you (yes, you) by name: "Come on _____ (your name). Come to Me. Are you weary? I'll give you rest. There's rest here. There's hope here. I love you."

Now I ask you, who wouldn't want to know a God like that? Beats me. Do *you?* You can. While God has provided a million (or two or three) ways to care for His people (namely, His angels), He has provided only one way (namely, Jesus Christ) for you to know Him—several ways to serve you, only one way to save you.

"Salvation comes no other way; no other name has been or will be given to us by which we can be saved, only this one" (Acts 4:12, *The Message*)—Jesus. Even if the angels can't figure that one out, you can. You have the tools. It's how you were created. God gave you an intellect to assess and evaluate His salvation plan for you. He gave you emotions to motivate and embellish the process. He gave you a will to choose to change direction in your life, to follow and accept Him.

He also gave you self-awareness, the ability to step back and see yourself as a creature somehow incomplete without Him in your life; as someone who struggles with the paradoxes of life, yearning for the ideal, yet struggling in the real; as someone who (if you're honest) realizes really just how far you must fall short of His ideal of holiness and wholeness; as someone who, despite your obvious shortcomings, still desperately wants to be accepted by Him anyway, forgiven by Him anyway, befriended by Him anyway.

Well, that's the kind of God He is. Take a step toward Him, will you?

Job Description of an Angel, Part I

You've got to remember,
you're not alone in this world.
Always remember,
you're not alone in this world. Never alone, never alone.
—DENNIS MORGAN

MY BROTHER-IN-LAW knows he is not alone in this world. Living in Ambato, Ecuador, he and his young family headed out one evening to visit friends. They found themselves cruising along at sixty-five miles per hour on a beautiful new stretch of the Pan-American Highway. All of a sudden the asphalt ended with no sign or warning and the Land Rover™ catapulted from the smooth surface onto dirt, skidding out of control toward a sharp curve directly in front of them.

Instinctively, he cranked the wheel to the left—dust flying, car sliding. After several seconds of feeling somehow momentarily suspended in flight, the vehicle came to rest thirty feet from the curve.

After a trip behind some nearby bushes, the family returned to discern how they had missed rolling the vehicle with that kind of momentum. To their horror, they discovered more than a curve with a ditch. The curve had a sharp, 300-foot drop off a steep cliff into a canyon below.

They charted the tracks of the Land Rover™ in the dirt as it was headed straight over the cliff. The track of the right front tire totally disappeared over the edge only to return several meters later back on the road. No natural explanation. Only this one:

> For he will command his angels
>> concerning you
> to guard you in all your ways;
> they will lift you up in their hands,
> so that you will not strike your foot
>> against a stone.
>> (Psalm 91:11–12)

In the last chapter we established that angels most surely exist and that they mingle betwixt and between the visible and the invisible worlds. Perhaps even as you read you are beginning to perceive where, how and why angels may have been involved in your own life.

Angels are all around us. Though we cannot see them, they are mingling about us in a dimension we cannot comprehend. But what are they doing? What does a day in the life of an angel really look like? What would be an angel's job description? Well, let's look at one.

JOB DESCRIPTION FOR THE POSITION OF HOLY ANGEL
Purpose Statement (General)

"All angels shall be ministering spirits sent out to render service for the sake of those who will inherit salvation" (Hebrews 1:14).

Purpose Statement (Detailed)

1. *All angels shall be "spirits."* One of several hundred billion uniquely created by God sometime before the creation of human beings. Each holy angel shall be unique with its own intellect, emotions and will.

Fallen or unholy angels or demons need not apply. Having exercised their free will to rebel against God, they and their leader Lucifer have no place in this invisible army.

2. *All angels shall be "ministering spirits," to God first and people second.* You will do things for human beings, but only on God's behalf. You will have no right or ability to act independently of God's will, but will take all orders from God and do what He alone directs. There shall be no cosmic Lone Rangers in this invisible army.

3. *All angels shall be "sent forth" from God to execute His will in heaven and on earth.* Generally, you will be sent forth invisibly, but periodically you may materialize as the situation requires. Sometimes you will appear as a normal human being, usually a man (Genesis 18); other times as striking, powerful or terrifying beings (as in passages of Daniel and Revelation). But you will never appear as an animal or any other subhuman form.

4. *All angels shall be sent forth to render service "for the sake of those who will inherit salvation."* In other words, you will serve those who are followers of Jesus Christ or those who are destined to become His followers. However, as Scripture and history also demonstrate, you may also be called upon to minister to those who are not in the "household of faith." The purpose will often be to motivate people to saving faith as a result of your encounter. But primarily, holy angels will be responsible for taking care of Christians. When human beings choose to receive Jesus Christ as their personal Forgiver, Friend and Ruler of their lives, they also receive the guarantee of the protection and care of the angels.

Some of you will be assigned to certain believers and humans will refer to you as "guardian angels" (Matthew 18:10; Acts 12:15; Genesis 48:16; Daniel 10:21; 12:1). In some cases you will be teamed up with other angels to care for certain individuals or situations as the need arises (Psalm 91:11).

5. *All angels shall be sent out "to render service."* Your primary responsibility is to serve God by regularly worshiping Him. Your secondary responsibility will be to serve God by serving human beings. Upon divine request and dispatch, you will provide human beings with several practical services as detailed below.

Major Areas of Responsibility

1. *Angels serve by announcing or forewarning.** * Angels have delivered some pretty important messages over the years. Think of the life of Jesus. Before He was born, an angel appeared separately to both Joseph and Mary, announcing to them that Mary would have a son. Soon after Jesus was born, an angel again appeared to them and warned them that Herod would try to kill Jesus and that they should get out of town, which they did, by going to Egypt and escaping the massacre.

After Herod died, an angel appeared to them in Egypt announcing the end of the crisis and telling them they could return to their home.

A friend of mine works in a warehouse in a city several hours from mine. Last fall, while walking down an aisle created by several pallets stacked about twenty feet high, he had a foreboding sense that he should stop in his tracks, which he did. A spontaneous and casual conversation with a co-worker quickly erased the ominous feeling. Several seconds passed.

Then, boom! A whole section of pallets collapsed at the very spot where he, to the best of his calculations, would have been walking had he not stopped. He

---

* *See* Appendix One: "Angels Announcing and Forewarning" for personal stories on this theme.

would no doubt have been crushed. Did an angel forewarn him? Listen to the rest of the story before you judge.

A few months later, a vacation took me to his city. As I was driving down a main street, I stopped at a traffic light. Glancing at the car beside me, I caught the wave and smile of my friend. Our paths had not crossed in over three years. He motioned to a nearby coffee shop and we spent the next hour catching up on each other's lives.

As he shared many of his disappointments with me, it quickly became apparent that his life was not going well. Then he told me about the incident in the warehouse. It was clear that God had preserved his life in that situation so he could arrive at this point where he would finally see his need of outside help. He was a man "about to inherit salvation" because the Holy Spirit was working in his life and angels had "been sent forth to minister to him." That day he opened his life to Jesus and went away a changed man.

Was it just a coincidence in the warehouse that saved his physical life followed by a coincidence on a street that saved his eternal life? I don't think so. This one fits the biblical pattern much too well to be coincidence. Are not angels, after all, ministering spirits (known to forewarn) sent out to those who are about to inherit salvation?

2. *Angels serve by strengthening and encouraging physically, emotionally and spiritually.**

> [God] gave a command to the skies above
> and opened the doors of the heavens;
> he rained down manna for the people to eat,
> he gave them the grain of heaven.

---

* *See* Appendix Two: "Angels Strengthening and Encouraging" for personal stories on this theme.

> Men ate the bread of angels;
> > he sent them all the food they could eat.
> > > (Psalm 78:23–25)

The nation of Israel has just been rescued by the miraculous parting of the Red Sea. Finally freed of the heel-dogging Pharaoh, off they go, all 2 million of them in search of the Promised Land.

But the triumphant spring in their step quickly turns to a defeated shuffle. You can go on energy only so long before the empty stomach kicks in. Here they are, wandering around the desert, starving and complaining that there is no food.

Did you ever wonder what they ate? "God gave them the grain of heaven and men ate the bread of angels." Angel food cake!

Billy Graham tells the story of Captain Eddie Rickenbacker and the crew of his B-17 plane, which ran out of fuel and crashed in the Pacific Ocean. "And this part I would hesitate to tell," Rickenbacker recalled, "except that there were six witnesses who saw it with me. A gull came out of nowhere and lighted on my head. I reached my hand up very gently and killed him and then we divided him equally among us. We ate every bit, even the little bones. Nothing ever tasted so good."[1]

The gull strengthened their lives until help came. Through this experience, Rickenbacker became a follower of Jesus Christ. "I have no explanation except that God sent one of His angels to rescue us." Sometimes He sends cake…sometimes a seagull.

Angels are often sent to encourage physically, but also emotionally and spiritually as well. Or sometimes all three, as was the case for Elijah (1 Kings 19:3–9) and Jesus (Matthew 4:11).

Perhaps a boost of energy will fuel a weary body. Or a surge of hope will nurse some shattered emotions. Or clear thoughts suddenly realign or recalibrate destructive or wrong thinking.

Perhaps a timely and relevant verse springs from the pages of Scripture or a book and completely changes your whole direction or attitude.

Perhaps you run into just the right person at just the right time with just the right message. Or someone phones or drops a token of encouragement—a small gift, a bag of potatoes, an encouragement card.

Perhaps these are some of the reasons God tells us to trust Him with all our hearts and not to lean on our own understanding, and that if we acknowledge Him in all our ways, He will direct our paths (Proverbs 3:5–7).

We cannot always tell whether or not ministries like these are that of an angel, but these are the kind of things they do. God and angels are masters of serendipity. And I believe they are invisibly and purposefully involved in our lives more than we give them credit for.

3. *Angels serve by protecting and defending.** * About 500 hundred years before the birth of Jesus, Nebuchadnezzar, king of Babylon, besieged Jerusalem and took with him several captives. Among them were three of Israel's best young men, Shadrach, Meshach and Abednego, all of whom were soon appointed to high-level administrative positions in the Babylonian province.

Nebuchadnezzar really liked himself and one day he decided to stage an "I Appreciate Myself and So Will You Day." He had a ninety-foot image of gold crafted and set it up on the plain of Dura and commanded everyone to fall down and worship it or suffer death by combustion (Daniel 3:1–6).

The three young Jews were in a tight spot. They were successful immigrants, albeit forced ones. But they had assimilated into the Babylonian world and had it about as good as any slave could have it anywhere. But still they were Hebrews

---

* *See* Appendix Three: "Angels Protecting and Defending" for personal stories on this theme.

at heart and their reticence to acknowledge "Nebuchadnezzar Day" was difficult to hide.

Their crime was reported and they were brought before the king. They do not give him the answer he wants. Daniel 3:16–18 begins to record the amazing events as they unfold:

> O Nebuchadnezzar, we do not need to defend ourselves before you in this matter. If we are thrown into the blazing furnace, the God we serve is able to save us from it, and he will rescue us from your hand, O king. But even if he does not, we want you to know, O king, that we will not serve your gods or worship the image of gold you have set up.

Verses 19 and 20 tell us that Nebuchadnezzar was "furious" and "he ordered the furnace heated seven times hotter than usual and commanded some of the strongest soldiers in his army to tie them up and throw them into the blazing furnace."

The king's elite men were immediately fried by the blast, while Shadrach and friends just kind of strolled on in unabated and took up positions in the heart of the furnace roar.

> Then King Nebuchadnezzar leaped to his feet in amazement and asked his advisers, "Weren't there three men that we tied up and threw into the fire?"
>
> They replied, "Certainly, O king."
>
> He said, "Look! I see four men walking around in the fire, unbound and unharmed, and the fourth looks like a son of the gods." (3:24–25)

> So Nebuchadnezzar called them out, untouched, unsinged and unscented. No natural explanation. Only this one: "Praise be to the God of Shadrach, Meshach and Abednego, who has sent his angel and rescued his servants!" (3:28).

Angels can keep God's people from physical danger. "For he will command his angels concerning you to guard you in all your ways" (Psalm 91:11).

THE INVISIBLE SHIELD OF PROTECTION

Harley was a teacher at the Christian school, which is part of our church. Recently he resigned to work at a mission in a nearby city. Harley knows he's not alone in this world. Shortly after he arrived at the mission, he related to me the following encounter with a "sniffer."

A sniffer hallucinates wildly when under the influence of glue and his behavior becomes erratic and unpredictable. This young man was causing a great deal of disturbance in the lineup of people waiting for supper. Because those who are extremely intoxicated are not allowed to enter, Harley promised to bring the man some food after the line was through, which he did.

Spotting him still waiting some distance down the street, Harley went to offer him some bread and a word of encouragement. Then to Harley's shock, the very tall and intimidating young man spun on his heels. "I'm going to break your nose!" he seethed.

Harley extended his hand with the bread and said, "Here, take the bread."

"You're not Jehovah!" he retorted, to which Harley instinctively responded, "I serve the Lord Jesus Christ."

The man swung at Harley but his fist stopped about six inches from Harley's face and froze. He tried again. And again. But he could not seem to break through the invisible shield of protection that mysteriously surrounded the man who had come to help him. Meanwhile, a small group of the sniffer's gang had congregated.

"You can't touch me," Harley proclaimed confidently.

One minute passed. Another. And another. All the while, a trembling, spring-loaded fist was frozen inches from Harley's face, while the sniffer's buddies unsuccessfully taunted him to fight back: "Come on, man, you're embarrassing us!"

The sniffer lowered his fist, grabbed the food and ran into the alley. Then, without explanation, the gang members too retreated into the darkness like warriors into a New Hebrides jungle. Harley returned to the mission where an old street person who had witnessed the whole incident was waiting for him.

"What you doing mixin' with that bunch? They are one of the most feared and dangerous gangs in the city."

But Harley had felt absolutely no fear because he knew he could not be touched.

"Sounds like an angel," I said.

"No doubt about it," was his confident reply. "We're convinced they surround us and our mission. There is an invisible army protecting us."

God's angels protect. When I think about this in reference to my wife and children and the people in my church, when I realize that we are not alone in this world because God has His angels looking out for us, I do not worry as much. Neither does my niece.

LISA'S ANGEL

Several years ago my sister lived in Guayaquil, Ecuador with her husband and then five-year-old daughter Lisa. Nights were hot, humid and noisy in their fourth-floor apartment, making it difficult for a little person to fall asleep at night.

My sister contracted rheumatic fever and became completely bedridden. That meant that some nights, when her dad was out, little Lisa had to put herself to bed. It was complicated by the fact that she had always been afraid of the dark. Her daddy would leave the light on in her room and then turn it off when he got home.

This went on for several months, until one night her father came home and the light was off. He couldn't figure out who had switched it off. It was too high for Lisa to reach and her mother confirmed she had not been in the room.

The next morning Mommy asked, "How did you turn off your light last night, Lisa?"

"I didn't. Jesus did," came the reply. "The angel came and tucked me into bed last night and told me that he lived in darkness as well as light and he would be with me every night and I don't need to be afraid. Then he went over and turned off the light and I went to sleep."

Both parents were a bit skeptical at first, but they could not deny the obvious. From that night on Lisa's fear was totally gone. From that night on she not only wanted but demanded to go to bed with the light off!

4. *Angels Serve by Delivering.** "The angel of the LORD encamps around those who fear him, and he delivers them" (Psalm 34:7). Angels not only serve people by preventing trouble but also by delivering, rescuing or getting them out of it. Peter discovered this firsthand in the first century. Luke relates his amazing story in Acts 12.

This was not a safe time to be a Christian. King Herod had a Nebuchadnezzar complex and began arresting and persecuting Christians. Having killed James, one of their best, he proceeded to hunt down the rest. Peter was promptly arrested and placed under heavy guard to await trial. And up went the prayers of God's people. Acts 12:5–6 say: "So Peter was kept in prison, but the church was earnestly praying to God for him. The night before Herod was to bring him to trial, Peter was sleeping between two soldiers, bound with two chains, and sentries stood guard at the entrance."

Houdini wouldn't even touch this one. But God did. And that night, "an

---

* *See* Appendix Four: "Angels Delivering" for personal testimonies on this theme.

angel of the Lord appeared and a light shone in the cell. He struck Peter on the side and woke him up. 'Quick, get up!' he said, and the chains fell off Peter's wrists" (12:7).

A few minutes later, Peter is outside the prison walls, a free man. And poof! The angel disappears. Peter scratches his head: "Now I know without a doubt that the Lord sent his angel and rescued me from Herod's clutches..." (12:11).

Coming to his senses, he thinks to himself, "I better go tell my small group, let them know I'm free so they can stop praying for me!" He goes straight to the house where his friends are praying for him. Rhoda, the servant girl, answers his knock. Peeking through the security hole (a crack between two boards), she shrieks at the sight of Peter! Leaving him standing there she runs back inside announcing, "Peter is at the door!" (12:14).

They look up from prayer (for Peter) and the reply is classic: "You're out of your mind!" Her insistence is met with an even better one: "It must be his angel" (12:15). Here they are, praying around the clock and the answer to their prayer is at the door and they don't believe it!

Meanwhile, Peter is still outside hammering on the door to which they finally respond. "And when they opened the door and saw him, they were astonished" (12:16). I mean, how dare the Lord answer our prayer so quickly? Peter motioned for them to be quiet. Then he came inside and explained how God had answered their prayers by sending an angel to deliver him.

Everyone learned a very important lesson that night: One of the ministries of angels is the deliverance of God's people. It still is. Turn the page.

Job Description of an Angel, Part II

Y ORDER OF THE CHIEF LLAMA of a certain Tibetan community, Sundar Singh was thrown into a dry well that was used as a prison. With a lid over the top that was secured and locked, he was left to die at the bottom among the bones and rotting flesh of the other unfortunate victims. On the third night when he had been crying to God in prayer, he heard someone unlocking the lid, and a voice spoke telling him to take hold of a rope that had been lowered. He did so and was glad to find a loop at the bottom of the rope in which he could place his foot, his arm having been broken when he was thrown down. He was then strongly pulled up and the lid was replaced and relocked. But when he looked around in the dark to thank his rescuer, there was no one to be seen. When morning came, Singh returned to the city in which he had been arrested and began preaching again. News came fast to the chief lama, who denied that it could have happened since the only key was attached to his own belt.[1]

SOUNDS A LOT LIKE what happened to Peter, doesn't it? God delivered. God delivers now. David Mitchell concurs. In his own words, he relates some unusual events that have gradually and fully convinced him of this reality—God sometimes chooses to dispatch angels to deliver, rescue and save people from danger.

Angels were always mysterious and mythical to me in my early days as a minister. An elderly clergyman once spoke critically of Sir Basil Spence's angels depicted on the huge glass doors of the postwar reconstructed Coventry Cathedral.

"Who's ever seen an angel like that?" he asked mockingly.

"Who's ever seen an angel?" I replied.

Well, I have learned a lot since then. I have met people who have seen angels and could describe their appearance and relay their words. And I have seen an angel at work, though he remained invisible. It happened like this.

Our daughter Helen was five years old at the time. Delphine and I, with our four young children, were on a post-Easter vacation in the English county of Gloucestershire. Delphine's mother, who was also with us, stopped to talk with someone and, while we were waiting, Helen drifted away to the vacant parking lot of an ancient stone inn.

Watching her closely, I suddenly saw her stumble forward, her head and arms flying backward as if she had been shoved abruptly from behind.

"Daddy, someone pushed me!" she cried, running toward me and clinging to my leg. Just then, a huge stone from the inn's centuries-old chimney broke loose and crashed down on the very spot where Helen had been standing just a few seconds before.

Every skeptical grain in my soul was swept away in that moment. I knew what I had seen with my own eyes.

Some time later I had opportunity to relate this story.

It was November 1965, and the rain was sheeting down as a west wind came driving up the English Channel. Seven men had gathered for fellowship in the vestry of St. Aidan's Church in Ernesettle, a suburb of Plymouth, Devon. The church served a parish of about 6,000 people living in a postwar municipal development.

"Vicar," said the stocky ex-petty officer Vic Selway, "do you believe in angels?" I replied that I certainly did and recounted the story I just told you. "I believe there are many occasions when angels intervene for God's children, just as it says in Hebrews 1:14: 'Are not all angels ministering spirits sent to serve those who will inherit salvation?'"

The men sat quietly for a moment or two, then began recounting their own personal stories that could possibly be explained by the presence of angels. The most memorable was that of Fred Train.

Fred was a warm, friendly man who seemed to know everyone. His face was always alight with a big smile. He was strong yet gentle and seemed to spend all his spare time serving others.

Not only was he a pillar of strength in the church, he also ran a large city-sponsored youth group in the park behind my vicarage. I knew Fred had a powerful influence on many youngsters who would probably not have been caught dead in a church.

"It was like this," he said. "During the war I served on a destroyer and got pretty close to all the men. There wasn't a man on that ship I didn't know." *I can understand that,* I thought. *Fred is that kind of man.*

"The terrible day came," Fred continued, "when we were torpedoed in the

Atlantic. The order came to abandon ship. She was listing sharply. I was sliding down the deck toward my lifeboat station when a matelot (sailor) with a big black beard grabbed me.

"'Fred,' he said, 'you've forgotten your grandfather's Bible!' My granddad had given me his Bible in the hope that I would read it. I never had. In fact, I never even opened it. But I did treasure it and kept it tucked away in my locker. So, before I knew what I was doing, I found myself scrambling back up the deck to get the Bible.

"When I got back to the lifeboat station, my boat had gone. I had just time enough to pile into the last lifeboat. We were pulling away from the ship when another torpedo passed close by us and hit a lifeboat already in the water. It was blown to smithereens. Vicar," he continued, "that was the boat I was supposed to have been in."

Fred paused briefly.

"The funny thing is that not one member of the crew knew I had a Bible. And," Fred swallowed and tears glistened in his eyes, "I had never seen that sailor before in my life!"

Wow! I hear stories like this and I have two reactions. First, it is exciting to know that as a follower of Jesus Christ I can never get myself in a situation that God cannot get me out of, if that is what He chooses to do.

But there is another reaction that none of us can avoid and it comes in the form of a question most of us have entertained at one time or another: "If that's true, if God protects, delivers and defends His people, where were the angels when such and such happened?"

I don't have a single, definitive answer to that one. No one does. But I have some ideas. Consider just three, which might help you put these haunting thoughts into some kind of understandable perspective.

WHERE WERE THE ANGELS WHEN...?

First of all, the answer to "Where were the angels when...?" is: "They were probably there...ministering in some way other than we might desire or recommend or comprehend or consider." God does not always respond according to our prescription. He alone knows the big picture and determines the extent to which He will respond to our little ones (or big ones).

A woman asked: "Where were the guardian angels when my daughter was stabbed to death?" The reply: "I believe they may have been with her, taking away the pain after the first wound."

Obviously, only sometimes do angels intervene miraculously in our lives. Why, I do not know. More often than we realize though, angels are doing their unseen work on a regular day-to-day basis, which we never recognize. Perhaps a better question is: "Why don't we start noticing how often they do minister and we don't take notice, instead of dwelling on how often they don't minister and we do take notice?"

Rescuing and ministering are two different things. God has not promised to deliver us from all disease, pain, suffering and adversity, but He does promise to be with us in the face of the worst of each.

Secondly, we must realize that we live in the physical realm not the spiritual one. Angels may not fall out of trees and break legs, but we do. It would be nice if we could fly without crashing, float without sinking and ski without wiping out. But we live in a fallen, physical world. And things are bound to happen.

A figure skater once remarked, "Angels can fly because they defy the laws of gravity." But we cannot. We are subject to the physical realm and God's laws of gravity that govern it. Now, sometimes at His own discretion, God chooses to override those laws and intervene supernaturally. Which leads us to a third consideration, the sovereignty of God.

WHY DOES GOD CHOOSE TO INTERVENE?

"Why does God choose to intervene at all?" He doesn't have to. Unquestionably God can and does provide and dispatch His angels from time to time, knowingly or unknowingly to people, but not all the time or as many times as we would like. On earth the ministry of angels is sporadic and unpredictable at best. Experience and Scripture are clear on that.

However, Scripture is also clear on something else and here is where hope and confidence is derived. It will not always be this way for the follower of Jesus Christ. The ultimate salvation and restoration of his or her physical body and the "rescue" from this physical earth is imminent!

The Bible says that when we die, we will have heavenly bodies similar to the angels'. And we will inhabit the same dimension as they do, heaven—a place where there will be no accidents or pain; where we will not run into each other and where, as the apostle John assures us (Revelation 21:4), God will wipe away every tear because there is no disappointment; where there will be no more death because we will live forever; where there will be no more mourning because there is no conflict, no more crying because there is no hurt, no more pain because there are no more accidents.

Until then, however, we live with the tension that, although it is our right and privilege to expect some measure of assistance in advance of that day, God in His mysterious sovereignty retains the decisive veto on what, where, when, why, how much and how often.

We must accept this truth, perplexing though it may be, trusting that whether through the ministry of His angels to us or not, His grace will be sufficient regardless of the situation and that all things really will work together for good to those who know and love God and are called according to His purpose (Romans 8:28).

He giveth more grace when the burdens grow greater;
He sendeth more strength when the labors increase,
To added affliction He addeth His mercy;
To multiplied trials, His multiplied peace.

His love has no limit; His grace has no measure;
His power has no boundary known unto men.
For out of His infinite riches in Jesus,
He giveth, and giveth, and giveth again

When we have exhausted our store of endurance,
When our strength has failed ere the day is half done,
When we reach the end of our hoarded resources,
Our Father's full giving is only begun.

—ANNIE J. FLINT (1862–1932)

5. *Angels serve by being active in answering prayer.** If you have read any of the popular literature on angels these days, you will discover a lot of confusion on this point. Suffice to say that the likes of Ask Your Angels is a "red-flag" title. "When you ask your angels," write its authors, "you can be sure that you will be answered."

In a book ((*Your Guardian Angels*) that claims to reveal "how to ask for help from your angels and be open to their guidance," author Linda Georgian even offers several sample prayers to angels.

Oh? Will they work?

According to the Bible—no! Unless you want fallen angels to respond. Scripture gives clear instructions on who to ask and how to ask. John 15:16

---

* *See* Appendix Five: "Angels and Prayer" for personal stories on this theme.

records Jesus' statement that "the Father will give you whatever you ask in my name."

Ask who? God the Father. Ask how? In Jesus' name. If you go directly to an angel via prayer on your own or through any other outside source or practitioner (channelers, mediums and the like), the angel you contact will not be from God.

Nowhere in Scripture does anyone under any circumstances pray directly to an angel, but always to God, who in turn, as He determines, may or may not choose to dispatch one or several angels to minister on His behalf. God is the Provider. He disperses the messengers. He is the "cosmic air traffic controller." Go straight to the source!

Remember the story of Peter in prison? An angel was involved in answering the prayer for his release. But look at verse five of Acts 12:5: While Peter was in prison, "the church was earnestly praying for him." To whom? To God. Not the angel. The angel didn't respond because Peter summoned the angel. The angel responded because God summoned the angel to deliver Peter on His behalf. That is the sequence. That is the formula. That is the only pattern.

So, how does it work? Ever wondered? Well, it is not prayer itself that "works" necessarily, but God who works in response to our prayer. So how does He work? You close your eyes, bow your head, talk to God…and things happen— mysterious, sometimes supernatural things.

You know that prayer is a place where burdens change shoulders. So you go to God with some heavy weights and, lo and behold, He lightens your load.

You are painfully aware of sin in your life. So you ask God to forgive you. You open your eyes and you somehow feel clean and light.

You are in danger. You cry to God for help and He delivers you. It was a miracle.

You worship God by praising Him and thanking Him and adoring Him. You rise up and somehow feel a new intimacy and kinship with your Creator.

You petition God for something. Perhaps you have lost your keys or a valuable ring. You pray for a job. A lost child. They are found. How did that happen?

You intercede for someone who needs healing or encouragement. They begin to mend and improve. You are amazed at the presence, power and pathos of God. But how did He do it?

Even though we may not understand the metaphysics involved, many people have repeatedly been impressed with the incredible power of prayer. It works. He works. But how and why is a mystery. It's like the foreign car I drive. Have you ever looked under the hood of one? Mine looks like a metal granny knot. So, rather than try to understand it, I just turn the key and drive. I have faith it will perform and it does (most of the time). Prayer is like that. God works through ours even though we may not know how. But let's speculate anyway.

In the theater of your imagination, picture two worlds: a physical, visible one and a spiritual, invisible one. Now, here's what prayer is. Prayer is someone in the physical world communicating with Someone in the spiritual one. Prayer is accessing the supernatural power of God to intervene in physical life and effect change there. Prayer somehow unlocks the doors to heaven and releases the Spirit of God and His angelic messengers to accomplish His work on earth. Psalm 103:19–21 confirms this:

> God has set his throne in heaven;
> he rules over us all. He's the King!
> So bless God, you angels, ready to hear
> and do what he says
> Bless God, all you armies of angels,
> alert to respond to whatever he wills.
> (*The Message*)

Think of it! An eager army of angelic messengers, spring-loaded around the throne of God just waiting to be released in answer to your prayers. Imagine the effect "praying without ceasing" would have on a life, a world or a church if we really believed this. Just being aware of this reality should bolster your faith and intensify your desire to pray more confidently, and more often.

Again, here is what can happen when you begin to pray. The prophet Daniel was good enough to let us in on a little something he saw, which should amaze you. One day while he was praying he saw an angel come to him in swift flight. Here is what the angel said: "Daniel, I have now come to give you insight and understanding. As soon as you began to pray, an answer was given, which I have come to tell you, for you are highly esteemed" (Daniel 9:22–23).

In the next chapter, he received a similar response to another prayer. The angel says: "Do not be afraid, Daniel. Since the first day that you set your mind to gain understanding and to humble yourself before your God, your words were heard, and I have come in response to them" (10:12).

Angels have a lot to do with prayer. Not everything, but a lot. God may choose to send angels in response as He did in Daniel's case or He may choose to respond Himself or through His Son Jesus or by His Holy Spirit (Romans 8:26). It's a big topic, but one thing is for sure, the angels are always ready and willing to respond. And sometimes it doesn't take much.

FEATHERS, LORD!

Surely he will save you from the
    fowler's snare
    and from the deadly pestilence.
He will cover you with his feathers,
    and under his wings you will find refuge.
                    (Psalm 91:3–4)

A good friend of mine likes to tell the fascinating story of a woman confronted by a band of thugs in a dark alley. The obvious emergency of the situation and her poor recall of a Bible verse learned years earlier left her with only a vague memory of something to do with "wings" and "protection," but that was all. Now cornered in the "fowler's snare," she faced certain injury, even death. Just as the men were upon her, she blurted out a panicked shriek: "Feathers, Lord! Feathers!" The faces of the would-be attackers were instantly etched with horror. They released their grip and ran terrified from the hapless but grateful woman.

"As soon as you began to pray, an answer was given." Tell me, why don't we pray more often?

Angels, where ere we go,
Attend our steps whate'er betide.
With watchful care their charge attend,
And evil turn aside.

—CHARLES WESLEY

6. *Angels serve by attending our deaths.* In other words, angels are there when it counts the most.*

"The time came when the beggar died and the angels carried him to Abraham's side [heaven]." (Luke 16:22)

The gift of comfort is a powerful theme in angel stories. Angels are busy when you die. Sometimes, as death draws near, a person catches a glimpse of angels and of the glory beyond.

A close family friend of ours was slowly passing away several years ago. My

---

* *See* Appendix Six: "Angels and the Dying" for personal stories on this theme.

father visited her often and the family kept a watchful vigil by her side. The last visit was the special one. Everyone knew she was very low and would not make it through the night.

At one point, her eyes fluttered. Sensing a momentary awareness, my father squeezed her hand. It startled her and she awoke ever so briefly only to whisper what caught her cloudy eyes in the room: "Look, there's Jesus...and the angels. Can't you see Him...right there?"

Everyone looked expectantly in the direction of her gaze. Nothing.

"No, we can't."

A faint smile creased her dry lips. She closed her eyes. She was gone.

How would you like to die with a smile on your face and with a host of friends in high places beckoning you home? How would you like to die with that kind of hope? You can. For the believer in Jesus Christ, the afterlife does not have to be terrifying. The transition might be. Dying itself might be. Let us not kid ourselves. We all want to get to heaven but no one wants to die to get there.

But for the believer death is a door to eternal peace and the angels will carry us over the threshold into the presence of God Himself. Throughout history, the appearance of angels at death has happened with great frequency.

In *Pilgrim's Progress* (1678), John Bunyan's wonderful allegory of the Christian life, Christiana asks Mercy why she is laughing in her sleep. "Were you dreaming?" she wonders aloud. Indeed she was—about her own death. Mercy herself thought it odd to laugh about that, but went on to describe to Christiana the beautiful side of it:

> Then I looked up and saw one with wings, coming toward me. I thought
> he came to me and said, "Mercy, what ails you?" And when he heard my

complaining, he said, "Peace be to you!" and wiped away my tears with his handkerchief, and clothed me in purple and gold. He put a golden chain about my neck, earrings on my ears, and a glittering crown upon my head. Then he took me by the hand and said, "Mercy, come with me." So we went up and up till we came to a pearly gate. After he knocked, the gate was opened, and we went in. I followed him up to a throne upon which One sat in splendor, Who said to me, "Welcome, daughter!"[2]

When they [God's people] arrive at the gates of death, GOD welcomes those who love him. (Psalm 116:15, *The Message*)

RECAP: We are not alone in this world. Angels are all about us. And they have a very specific and detailed job description. And they are doing a very good job. And if you are "one who is about to inherit salvation," you have probably noticed that God's angels are watching over you too.

The Bible is clear: God's people are guaranteed the ministry of angels in this present life. You can also expect the ministry of angels in the transition from this life to the next. And you can expect and anticipate spending the rest of eternity in the presence of those angels and the God who made you—and them. Friends in high places—you need never leave home without them.

Now that should put a lump in your throat and a smile on your face. This is happy stuff. Now that we've got you there, perhaps this is as good a time as any to shift gears and explore in the following chapter the other side of this teaching—the sad stuff. Because, unfortunately, there is some and you need to hear about it too—what we might call "enemies in low places," or as St. Augustine distinguished them:

There are, then, spiritual forces
    of wickedness
on high, not where the stars glimmer
    in orderly
array and the holy angels abide, but in the
murky abode of the lowest region of the air,
where the mist is collected...."
(*Sermons on the Liturgical Season,* Fathers of the Church, Inc., 1959)

The Rise and Fall
of a Beautiful Angel

Tom: I remember one summer I had a whole bunch of rabbit's feet…just to ensure I'd come home from Camp Chungkawalawala alive.

Diane: Real rabbit's feet?

Tom: Real rabbit's feet from Korvers' Five and Dime, the only kind that worked, right, Jeff?

Jeff: (laughing) I remember I once used a rabbit's foot for casting a spell.

Marge: You're kidding? What kind of a spell?

Jeff: I think it was so that Mary Sue Smits would break out in chronic acne!

Marge: Those were the days!

Diane: Yeah, but nowadays you read about really evil, even demonic things that kids are into. That's what bothers me.

Tom: I think a lot of that stuff is overblown. The media always plays up the sensational stuff. There's nothing to it.[1]

Nothing to it?
Two little boys were having a little-boy discussion one day.

"There's no real devil," pronounced one conclusively.

"I know," agreed the other. "It's just like Santa Claus. It's your father." It would be even funnier if he was not serious. Our culture tends to put Santa and Satan on the same fairy tale level.

It was the French poet Baudelaire who said: "The devil's cleverest ruse is to make men believe that he does not exist. That there's 'nothing to it.'"

C.S. Lewis, in his masterful book *The Screwtape Letters*, documents the fictional correspondence between two demons, Uncle Screwtape and his underling student, Wormwood. Wormwood, it seems, is concerned that he is losing one of his "patients" to Christianity. At one point, Screwtape offers the following advice:

I do not think you will have much difficulty in keeping the patient in the dark. The fact that "devils" are predominantly comic figures in the modern imagination will help you. If any faint suspicion of your existence begins to arise in his mind, suggest to him a picture of something in red tights, and persuade him that since he cannot believe in that, he therefore cannot believe in you.[2]

Well, according to a poll by *TIME* magazine (December 27, 1993) Screwtape, Wormwood and company have been every successful. They have at least half of us convinced. While sixty-nine percent of people surveyed seem to have no trouble believing in the existence of angels, only forty-nine percent believed that some of them are fallen angels or demons.

BLACK AND WHITE FEATHERS

Many of us don't like to think about a real devil. So we don't, much. And when we do (if we do), we tend to just sluff the notion off with a kind of amused tolerance: "Ah, there's nothin' to it."

The trouble is, the Bible says there is a lot to it, so much so that if you choose to deny the existence of a real devil and his angels, you will have to deny God and His angels because both are presented as existing, personal beings in Scripture. Flip through the pages of your Bible and you will hear the rustle of black as well as white feathers.

In fact, as early as the third chapter of the first book (Genesis), one of them is ruffling snake's skin, not plumage. Now if that doesn't sound like the kind of angel we have been talking about so far, it's because he is not.

Sometime before the creation of human beings, something macabre and horrific happened in heaven. A large group of angels rebelled (Revelation 12:7–9). And since that day, there have been two types of angels: holy angels who have remained obedient to God and carry out His will to this day, and unholy or fallen angels (demons) who disobeyed God, lost their holy condition and until this day oppose and hinder God's work.

We have spent the first several chapters talking about the former group and have been encouraged by the reality that God has an invisible army of powerful and unseen holy agents poised to minister to us in our need. But that is only part of the picture. No discussion on angels is complete without considering both sides of reality. The story of the rise and fall of a beautiful angel is the second side—a tragic one with lethal implications for those who choose not to believe it.

We began our discussion of angels by making a case for the existence of holy angels. Let's do the same for the fallen variety. You can decide how much there is to it. Be warned, however, that these truths are infinitely less palatable even if they are just as surely, accurately and poignantly documented in the same Bible. And remember:

> *The first trick of the devil is incognito. God*
> *says, "I am who I am." The devil says, "I am no-*
> *body. What are you afraid of? Are you going to*
> *tremble before the nonexistent?"*
>
> —DENIS DE ROUGEMENT
> *("La Part du Diable")*

Well, are you? You need not even if he is existent (which he is). Let's see why.

WHO SAYS THERE IS A REAL DEVIL?

Is the devil real? Or, like Santa Claus or the Easter Bunny, a figment of culture's fantasy or our imagination? Is there a personal, active, living, invisible angelic rebel leader of myriads of fellow fallen cohorts cohabitating the same universe as holy angels and opposing their leader God as we speak? Or is there "'nothin' to it"? Is there a real devil and, if so, who says so?

OUR REASON SAYS SO

When you stop to reflect on the world we live in, reason alone indicates there must be an adversary out there not willed by God. Think about it. There is a perfect, self-existent, all-knowing, all-present, all-powerful God who creates an invisible spirit world in the heavenlies. He then proceeds to create a visible, physical universe and world, and a perfect one at that. But look around, folks. Something obviously has happened to both worlds! Because absolute peace and harmony do not exist in either. Instead, "There is a puzzling dichotomy of happiness and sorrow, of wisdom and stupidity, of fulfillment and failure, of kindness and cruelty, of life and death."[3]

Operating in our world there are two diametrically opposed forces constantly running friction against each other. Tell someone, "God loves you and has a wonderful plan for your life" and a likely response might be, "Oh really? Well, where was God when our daughter died or we lost our business or a hurricane destroyed our home?" The fact that there is obvious opposition to God and goodness in our world indicates the very real presence of a hostile power not willed by God, who is actively and purposefully engaged against Him. The Bible clearly identifies the culprit as Satan.

Why? How did this happen? How could God *let* it happen? You are not the first one to scratch your head over this one. Even the apostle Paul, brilliant as he was, referred to this dilemma as the mystery of iniquity or the secret power of lawlessness (2 Thessalonians 2:7). To this day, people who study God for a living, brilliant as they are, have had to invent a name for it—theodicy, i.e., things that confuse even theologians, like, where did evil come from if a perfect God is the originator of everything? Why would, could, did a good God create bad? Why would one angel who "had it made" decide to rebel? Where did the seed of rebellion come from? Somewhere outside of him? How, if there was no other evil in the universe? Did his temptation come from within? How, if there was no sin in any of the angels? Where did it come from then?

Better put that one on your "when I get to heaven I'm going to ask" list, because God hasn't revealed this to us yet. But it happened. That we know. Reason says so. Maybe Scripture doesn't give us all the answers to the origin of humanity's problems, but it does give the answer to the results of all of them. More on that later. For now, who or what else says there is a devil?

THE BIBLE SAYS SO

Almost every contributing author to the Bible assumed, believed, spoke or wrote about the devil. Just for starters, consider a sampling. First John 3:8 tells us Satan has been sinning from the beginning. And so he has, tempting Eve in

Genesis 3, Job throughout the whole book of Job, Jesus in Luke 4, and Judas in Luke 22. He rises up against Israel in First Chronicles 21, hinders God's servants in First Thessalonians 2 and has power over others in Acts 10. He ensnares the wicked in First Timothy 3 and deceives the nations in Revelation 20.

Matthew 4 finds him misinterpreting, perverting and abusing God's Word. Jude 6, opposing God's angels and Matthew 13, hindering God's gospel.

He walks about as a roaring lion in First Peter 5, disguises himself as an angel of light in Second Corinthians 11 and a snake in Revelation 20. He is the accuser of believers in Revelation 12. He has power of death in Hebrews 2. And the whole world lies in his lap in First John 5.

Is the devil real? According to the Bible he is very real. It is also pretty obvious when you look at the society we live in. The telltale cultural evidence is equally copious and convincing.

Our Culture Says So

Screwtape: "I wonder you should ask me, [Wormwood], whether it is essential to keep the patient in ignorance of your own existence. Our policy, at least for the moment, is to conceal ourselves."[4]

I think the policy is changing. The overt escalation and display of evil in just the last few years alone makes it quite clear that Screwtape and company are out of the closet. The lead lines of a feature article I read on Satan this summer ditto these sentiments:

> You can feel the heat, can't you? No, it's not just summer, it's not global warming. Wake up and smell the burning, scorching, scalding, unholy hot coffee, you fools! It's the Devil! Beelzebub! Diabolus! Lucifer! Don't you see? He's everywhere. He is at work among us, more than ever—tempting us, leading us astray, selling us stuff we don't need. He is irritating, terrifying,

ubiquitous—the Kathy Lee Gifford of the Underworld—and he's working double time, fitting ever more appearances into his busy, sinister schedule. He's on TV, he's in bookstores, he's featured on the album covers of semi-popular bands. It's hard not to feel engulfed by his dark and fiery presence.[5]

Just take a stroll down the aisle of your favorite local bookstore, comic shop or video outlet. Flip through the channels on your television set on Saturday morning! I mean, when Walt Disney cannot even produce a full-length animated feature without building the most hideous creatures imaginable into the plot, when children (mine, at least) have nightmares about wizards in Care Bears of all things, when the mayor of Los Angeles sponsors a Freddy Krueger Day to honor a demonic slasher from a cinematic nightmare, in a day when some people are so obviously convinced he exists that they overtly and openly worship him, we have to admit that the cultural evidence is staggering.

His recognizable and provocative graffiti litters our planet. Satan on skateboards. Satan on beer labels ("Faust," Anheuser-Busch's latest "brew"). Satan in Nike's European soccer ads. Satan on hockey jerseys (New Jersey Devils). Satan at ski resorts: "Go to Heaven, ski like Hell."

These days, Satan sells. As the saying in the industry goes, "Before you sell something to someone, you have to tempt them. Who better to do the tempting."[6] Says Rob Reilly, an ad copywriter, "Today, evil sells. Sex has been overdone, it's run its course. Evil and Satan are the hot things right now."[7]

Is the devil real? Manufacturers would like us to think so, and many are using him to make a statement that their product is the "rebellious" thing to eat, drink or wear.

Culture says there is a real devil. But even more convincing is something I call heart evidence.

OUR HEARTS SAY SO

There is something in the heart of all of us that knows something is wrong with our world. Something is out of whack in our own hearts. We know the things we are capable of doing, thinking, planning, scheming in our own little shadows. Surely this is enough evidence to prove the existence of evil.

Even a child knows all is not right with this world. When it comes to good and evil, you do not have to cite chapter and verse to convince a three-year-old that both are very real. You don't have to educate a child to be afraid of the dark and things that go bump in the night. They know it instinctively. Nightmares can begin around eighteen months and fear chases all of us for the rest of our lives in one relative form or another.

My wife was having lunch in a local mall around Halloween time. Our then three-year-old daughter was very uneasy. She kept looking behind her, then at her mommy: "I don't like that man, Mommy. He's angry. He frightens me." My wife pivoted on her stool only to catch the hideous scowl of a large, stuffed warlock revolving center stage in the display area of the mall's long hallway.

They left, but the image went with them. Our daughter talked about it all day. And for several weeks thereafter, quite unannounced and at quite the unexpected times, she would say, "Don't like that man, Mommy. He frightens me." Where did she get that? That is not learned. That is instinctive. Even children know something is out of sorts in this world and that evil has something to do with it.

Now, by contrast, consider what happened that night. At bedtime, she began examining her room with a searching look accompanied by, "Where is Jesus, Daddy, Mommy?" Now three sets of eyes scan the room in unison until we all focus at the same time on a picture of Jesus knocking on the door of someone's heart.

"There is Jesus," she sighed with relief. "There's Jesus over there too!" Another picture of Jesus cradling a frightened lamb in his arms. "Jesus protects me, right, Mommy?" No fear. Where did she get that? Why did she instinctively fear the creature in the mall and naturally love the Shepherd on the wall? Heart evidence. (By the way, who would you trust instinctively? Jesus Christ, who first appeared to people on earth as a baby boy, the Son of God, or Lucifer, who made his debut as a snake? Just a thought.)

But there is more to consider.

OUR EXPERIENCE SAYS SO

Once when the great evangelist Billy Sunday was asked why he believed in a real devil, he responded, "There are two reasons. One, because the Bible says so; two, because I've done business with him."

Perhaps the most telltale evidence of all is the empirical—the observations of people whose experiences verified his existence. Angels can materialize or manifest themselves both for the purposes of God (Genesis 18:1-22; 19:1) or the purposes of Satan. But, in the same way that many of us will never actually see, feel, know or experience the activity of holy angels in our lives, neither will most of us see or be consciously aware of the actions of fallen angels either. However, many people do, have and will. For those, it is proof enough.

WHERE DID HE COME FROM?

Cherubim are angelic beings of the highest rank. They are indescribably beautiful and incomprehensibly powerful (2 Thessalonians 1:7). As protectors of God's holiness, they frequently appear surrounding His presence to worship and proclaim His magnificence (Ezekiel 10:1–22; Revelation 4:6–8).

Gabriel and Michael are the most recognizable cherubim, but did you know there was a third, perhaps even greater one than even they? The Bible introduces this "anointed cherub" in Isaiah 14:12: "How you are fallen from heaven, O Lucifer, son of the morning" (NKJV). The most glorious creature God ever created is one whom today we can barely stand to acknowledge even exists. It wasn't always that way.

> *Never was seen such an angel—eyes of heavenly blue, features that shamed Apollo, hair of golden hue.*
>
> —ROBERT SERVICE
> *(The Woman and the Angel)*[8]

And a beautiful name to go along with it—Lucifer. Believe it or not, you couldn't pick a more beautiful name in Hebrew than his. It means, "Son of the Dawn," "shining one," "star of the morning." What a gorgeous angel he was—the *magnum opus* of God's creation. He is described in all his original rise and glory in Ezekiel 28.

> You were the model of perfection,
>   full of wisdom and perfect in beauty . . .
> every precious stone adorned you:
>   ruby, topaz and emerald,
>   chrysolite, onyx and jasper,
>   sapphire, turquoise and beryl.
> Your settings and mountings were
>   made of gold;
>   on the day you were created they were
>   prepared.
> You were anointed as a guardian cherub,
>   for so I ordained you.

> You were on the holy mount of God;
> you walked among the fiery stones
> [God's shining glory]. (28:12–14)

This is his Creator speaking. And you can almost feel the heart-wrenching pathos in His voice as He speaks in the past tense of His own creation gone awry.

> You were blameless in your ways
> from the day you were created
> till wickedness was found in you.
> Through your widespread trade
> you were filled with violence,
> and you sinned.
> So I drove you in disgrace from the mount
> of God,
> and I expelled you, O guardian cherub,
> from among the fiery stones. (28:15–16)

If it weren't bad enough to be the genesis of evil itself (1 John 3:8), Lucifer then proceeded to spread it to those around him. He sold himself. He trafficked his pride and propagated his disobedience. He merchandised his rebellion and for some unknown reason he found some eager buyers. Actually, several. Revelation 12:3–4 indicates that he managed to attract one-third of the entire angelic host who likewise attracted God's wrath in the process. Quite a demotion—from the nucleus of God's shining glory to the center of a shopping mall! A bit overstated, but you get the point. "All the nations who knew you are appalled at you; you have come to a horrible end and will be no more" (Ezekiel 28:19).

How did he and they who had such glorious beginnings come to such horrible ends? The Old Testament prophet Isaiah asked the same question (Isaiah 14:12) and provides our answer.

THE FALL OF A BEAUTIFUL ANGEL

"How you have fallen from heaven, O morning star, son of the dawn! You have been cast down to the earth, you who once laid low the nations!" (Isaiah 14:12).

Considering who they were and where they were and what they did and the price they paid, you have to somehow feel sorry for them. How the original temptation to rebel was ever even generated in Lucifer's heart in the first place is beyond anyone. How it was ever reciprocated by others in the second place is beyond everyone. But it was, and they did, and Isaiah 14:13 explains why, if not how: "You said in your heart, 'I will'..."

The shortest definition of sin is "I will." Sin is choosing your will over God's will. You don't have to trace any sin very far before you will discover at its root some form of pride. Pride was the seminal root in the first five sins ever committed. Since then, all other sins are just a variation on the same theme. Here is a list of those first five sins paraphrased from Lucifer's own words (Isaiah 14:13–14):

1. "I will ascend to heaven"—I will occupy the throne of God.

2. "I will raise my throne above the stars of God"—I will take over as supreme ruler including the angels of God.

3. "I will sit enthroned on the mount of assembly"—I will be the center of God's kingdom rule.

4. "I will ascend above the tops of the clouds"—I will be above the glory of God.

5. "I will make myself like the Most High"—I will be God!

And God said, "No you won't!" Then Jesus, describing what happened next said, "I saw Satan fall like lightning from heaven" (Luke 10:18). When he fell, he fell fast! And his beauty was immediately corrupted and so was every angel that thought those thoughts in concert with him. In an instant, all were doomed to separation from God forever.

THE LANDING OF A BEAUTIFUL ANGEL

The rise was magnificent. The fall was cataclysmic. But just imagine the landing! Take the lid off your brain again and picture this celestial hailstorm of myriads of angelic beings pouring down from galactic recesses of an infinite universe and pelting onto earth. It would make a meteor shower look like a dew drop!

Donald Grey Barnhouse, referring to Satan's curse in Genesis 3:14 ("You will crawl on your belly and you will eat dust all the days of your life") said: "In that same moment Satan got his first mouthful of dust."[8] And he has been eating it ever since!

When Lucifer fell, he landed on an earth that was perfect, like he used to be. But his own evil ethic came with him and earth would never be the same. As soon as he picked himself up and brushed off, he took up here where he left off and quickly began merchandising his wickedness on the next easiest targets—human beings.

I do not know why God did not just speak a word and zap Satan and his cohorts out of existence. The Bible does not explain that (*theodicy*, remember?). But perhaps, as teacher/author John MacArthur has astutely observed, God chose to let the seed of rebellion run its gamut right to the end of time as we know it until it will be demonstrated to all beings and creatures once and for all that all things put together cannot and will not dethrone God. And then no one in the entire universe will ever again doubt that God's authority will ever be usurped.[9] By the way, that is exactly what is going to happen. But until that day, what is a fallen angel like now?

WHO IS LUCIFER NOW?

Well, Lucifer is still an angel—a corrupted one, but an angel nevertheless. And like every other angel, he has a personality (intellect, emotions and will), but his character is completely different. One way we know he has personhood is by observing his devices—his ability to make a plan, spin a plot, devise a trick, twist a truth, scheme a scheme.

Another evidence of his personality is his ability to communicate. He communed with Eve in Genesis, with God in the book of Job and with Jesus in Matthew. He also has the ability to exercise his own will and to choose. He desires certain things and directs his will in areas that he feels will fulfill that desire (Luke 4). Like all other created beings, Satan too is personally accountable to God. All these characteristics indicate personality.

But probably the most revealing thing of all is what emerges from the various names he is given in Scripture. And they are many!

When Lucifer hit earth, he got a name change before he landed for the second bounce. Actually, he got several. Even though he still likes to masquerade as Lucifer (angel of light) with an appearance of good, it is only wishful thinking. He may, as Elvis Presley theologized, "look like an angel...but he's the devil in disguise." He is no longer a star of the morning. He is not even a falling star. He is a fallen star. While the name Lucifer reflected who he once was—the "seal of perfection"—his new names reflect who he has now become.

Satan (adversary or opposer). Devil or *diabolos* (Greek, meaning one who slanders or trips up). Old Serpent (crafty, subtle, wily, deceitful, deceiving). Great Red Dragon (terrifying beast bent to destroy). Roaring Lion (one who devours). Evil One or *poneros* (one who delights in corrupting others). Destroyer or *abaddon* (Hebrew) or *apollyon* (Greek). Tempter (entices others to evil). Beelzebub (lord of flies).

Want some others titles? Accuser. Murderer. Liar. Father of Lies. Prince of this World. Prince of the Power of the Air. Prince of Demons. God of this Age.

Who is he now? we ask again. Well, what's in a name? More than just a dirty face, two horns, red tights, a pitchfork and a pillowcase full of candy, like the man who dressed up like this and on his way to a party got caught in a downpour. Conveniently, he slipped into the open door of a church where an old-time gospel meeting was in progress.

At the sight of the devil's costume, people began fleeing in terror for the exits, apparently forgetting James 4:7: "Resist the devil, and he will flee from *you*" (emphasis mine). Nevertheless, out they went, all of them except one poor woman whose coat was wedged on the end of a pew. As the "devil" came closer and closer, she pleaded: "Satan, I've been a member of this church for thirty years, but...but...but I've really been on your side all along!"

All of a sudden the devil became real to her. Yes, the devil is real. He is an angel, albeit a fallen one, a personal being with a very sinister agenda.

> One day the angels came to present themselves before the LORD, and Satan also came with them. The LORD said to Satan, "Where have you come from?"
>
> Satan answered the LORD, "From roaming through the earth and going back and forth in it." (Job 1:6–7)

Oh, yeah? And just exactly what were you doing?

What does a devil do anyway? What is the job description of an unholy angel?

Job Description of a Fallen Angel

PURPOSE STATEMENT (GENERAL):

ALL UNHOLY ANGELS shall do all the things your name(s) suggest and more. To put it succinctly, you shall do everything opposite to what holy angels do.

PURPOSE STATEMENT (DETAILED) PART I:

1. While holy angels minister to God at every turn, *fallen angels shall oppose God at every turn.*

2. While holy angels are sent forth to execute God's will, *fallen angels shall be sent forth to malign God's character.*

3. While holy angels render service to followers of Jesus Christ, *fallen angels shall attempt to wreak havoc on them and everyone else.*

4. While holy angels are sent forth to provide practical assistance, *fallen angels shall be sent forth for destruction.*

5. While holy angels are announcing or forewarning truth, *fallen angels shall be concealing, misleading and propagating lies.*

6. While holy angels strengthen, encourage and build up, *fallen angels shall try to weaken, discourage and tear down.*

7.   While holy angels are busy freeing and delivering, *fallen angels shall be busy enslaving and oppressing.*

8.   While holy angels assist in answering prayers, *fallen angels shall attempt to thwart prayers.*

9.   While holy angels are sympathetic at our deaths, *fallen angels shall take delight in death.*

At every point of good that God's angels render, there is a counterpoint reaction of evil. C.S. Lewis is right: "There is no neutral ground in the universe: every square inch, every split second is claimed by God and counterclaimed by Satan."[1]

There is an invisible battle constantly being waged in the invisible realm. Fallen angels are here right now contending for the hearts of men and women, even yours. Should you worry? Not if you are a follower of Jesus Christ. Greater is He that is in you (Jesus) than he that is in the world (Satan) and if you are a child of God, the battle is already won in and for your heart. You are on the winning side and whether you know it or feel it or not, your personal battles are just mopping up operations against a retreating enemy who has long since lost the war.

Do you believe that?

Believe it. It's true.

But to really put Satan in a proper perspective, we need to consider one final thing—who he is not. He is a whole lot less than we think and than what he would like to believe he is. He is a "wannabe." He and his angels are not God but they "wannabe." No angels are God. Satan is not self-existent—he was created like all the angels. He is a creature and is therefore limited and infinitely inferior to God. And although he will "wannabe" like God, he will "neverbe"—in several ways.

PURPOSE STATEMENT (DETAILED) PART II:

1. *All unholy angels will "wannabe" omniscient.* Satan and his angels are wise, even brilliant, but he and they do not know everything. Only God knows everything. You have only to look at Satan's track record to know that. He cannot read your thoughts and (this may come as a shock to some) he cannot tell your future. Just check out some of his popular devices and you will conclude he is a charlatan. And yet millions of people decide their daily actions by consulting one or more of his devices on a daily basis. Like a horoscope in the daily newspaper. Or a long distance phone call to a late-night psychic at $5 a minute! Or a crystal ball or fortune-teller. A tarot card reading, a channeler, a medium or the random movements on a ouija board. (Did you know that the word "ouija" is the combination of the word for "yes" in both French and German?)

In *The Invisible War*, Donald Grey Barnhouse notes that "the devil always says *yes, yes*, to his followers. They do not like No for an answer; therefore, they shall have *yes*."[2] Give them what will tickle their ears. Now you know why Jesus said, "Let your 'Yes' be 'Yes' and your 'No' 'No,'" because, as Matthew 5:37 goes on to warn, "...anything beyond this comes from the evil one." If all the devil says is yes, yes all the time, then at least one-half of what he says is a lie. And all of this, Barnhouse observes, "on the pretense of a being who has not the remotest inkling of what is going to take place tomorrow, other than what he can read in the prophecies of the Bible [which you can too] or can foresee in the manner of a good political commentator or columnist"[3] (which you can also do and, if you're an entrepreneur, get rich at it in the process).

I repeat, Satan does not know your future. He is not God. There is a picture of Geraldine Barr (Roseanne's sister) in *People* magazine sitting across from her fortune-teller. The caption is a fitting conclusion for us: "I loving getting tarot readings. They're always wrong." You are thinking what I am thinking, right? Why do it?

2. *All unholy angels will "wannabe" omnipresent.* But only God is everywhere present all the time. Angels have spatial limitations and literally have to move from place to place like any other being. They cannot be everywhere all the time. Now Satan—do not ever forget it—is like that and so are his angels. They are ubiquitous, but they are not everywhere. Only God fills infinity.

3. *All unholy angels will "wannabe" sovereign.* Call the shots. Be in control. Well, Satan may be the "prince of this world" but he does not have any more control over it than the One Sovereign God allows. Satan may very well rule a domain of fallen angels but he does not rule beyond them nor the confines God permits, namely this earth.

In fact, Satan never has been able to wrestle himself away from the controlling hand of God. His initial rebellion failed. His continued rebellion fails. To view him properly, then, picture him as one in exile. A dead one on furlough. One who has been expelled to earth and the domain around it to await final judgment. One who with his demon army, although free to roam to and fro about the earth (Job 1:7), continues, as John Calvin noted, to drag his chains wherever he goes (2 Peter 2:4; Jude 6).

4. *All unholy angels will "wannabe" winners.* Satan is a defeated foe, a convicted criminal on death row. Jesus Christ defeated him at the cross once and for all and it will just be a matter of time before his rebellion runs its limits, God steps in and Christ returns to earth to carry out the sentence passed centuries ago (2 Thessalonians 2:8).

> *So…a while he stood, expecting*
> *Their universal shout and high applause*
> *To fill his ear; when, contrary, he hears,*
> *On all sides, from innumerable tongues*

A dismal universal hiss, the sound
Of public scorn. He wondered, but not long
Had leisure, wondering at himself now more.
His visage drawn he felt to sharp and spare,
His arms clung to his ribs, he legs entwining
Each other, till, supplanted,
down he fell,
A monstrous serpent on his belly prone,
Reluctant, but in vain;
a greater power
Now ruled him, punished in
the shape he sinned,
According to his doom. He would have spoke,
But hiss for hiss returned with forked tongue
To forked tongue; for now were all transformed
Alike, to serpents all, as accessories
To his bold riot [revolt].

—JOHN MILTON,
(*Paradise Lost:* Book X)[4]

So there you have it. The story of the rise and fall of a beautiful angel. Kind of makes Darth Vader look like Pooh Bear, doesn't it? Not only that, *Star Wars* is fiction. This one is not. Every bit of it is true, recorded in graphic and disturbing detail in the pages of Scripture.

SO WHAT?

Even if you do (or are beginning to) believe there is something to it, so what? What difference can knowing any of this make to my life? The topic defines the conclusion. We cannot get around it. It is black and white. This information is more than just a story, or a myth. All the events actually happened and are happening. It is a true story, which contains propositional truth in story form and, as such, it demands a response from the hearer—a choice. You either accept it as the truth that it is and do something about it or you choose not to believe it and do nothing. It is your choice.

While you might be deciding, let me remind you of a couple of things. To deny the existence of this fallen angel leads also to a denial of the existence of God as He presents Himself in the Bible too. And to deny the existence of the true God is to deny the existence of pardon and forgiveness and salvation and hope and heaven. That denial will leave you in the midst of your own sin and the same fate as the fallen angels.

Those are the facts.

So, what are the choices?

Really, only two. To quote a great theologian—Bob Dylan: "It might be the devil or it might be the Lord, but you are gonna have to serve somebody."

In the Old Testament, Joshua said, "Choose for yourselves this day whom you will serve....As for me and my household, we will serve the LORD" (Joshua 24:15). In the New Testament, Jesus said, "No one can serve two masters....He who is not with me is against me" (Matthew 6:24; 12:30). It's just that cut and dried.

But you might be thinking, "Can't I waffle a bit longer while I think it over? I'm not 100 percent convinced there is a real devil. I'm not sure I really see a need for God yet."

No, you should not wait. And yes, you do need Him. You see, failing to choose is in itself a choice. There is no middle ground. You are making a choice whether you know it or not. It would be nice to ride the median on this one, but there is none.

So, which is it going to be—the fallen angel who bugles, "I am thy heaven, there is no other hope"? The prince of this world who brags, "There is no other world"? The tempter who bribes, "There is no judge"? The accuser who blabs, "There is no pardon"? The liar who bellows, "There is no evil. It is just an illusion. There is nothing to it"? The serpent who breathes, "I am nobody. What are you afraid of? Are you going to tremble before the nonexistent?"

Or God?

Jehovah God says, "I Am who I Am. The Alpha and Omega. The Beginning and the End. The First and Last." And Jesus, the Son of God, says,

I am the road, also the truth, also the life. No one gets to the Father apart from me. (John 14:6, *The Message*)

Look at me. I stand at the door [of your heart]. I knock. If you hear me call and open the door, I'll come right in and sit down to supper with you. Conquerors will sit alongside me at the head table, just as I, having conquered, took the place of honor at the side of my Father. That's my gift to the conquerors!

Are your ears awake? Listen [to me]. (Revelation 3:20-22, *The Message*).

There really isn't a choice. Let me appeal in closing this chapter by compressing it all into a few simple words even a three-year-old can comprehend: "What's it gonna be? The angry creature in the mall? Or the loving Shepherd on the wall?"

"Don't like that man, Daddy. I like Jesus. Jesus protects me, right, Daddy?"

You better believe it, kid! Far greater is He that is in you than he that is in the world.

Is He in you?

Old Angels in a New Age

I N HIS BOOK, *Dark Secrets of the New Age*, Texe Marrs paints this unusual scene:

> The seven hundred people packed into the Seattle auditorium have paid $400 each to hear Ramtha. They sit in excited expectation, their pulses pounding, their eyes rapturously cast upon the stage. Then Ramtha comes forth. He speaks marvelous words, exhorting the audience to know that each one of them is God and that nothing they do is evil, because there is no good and evil in human nature. He scorns the teachings of Jesus, cynically proclaiming that because each person is God, they do not need anyone else to teach them. Ramtha also reveals that "in the seed of Lucifer lies God and divineness."
>
> Hearing Ramtha's resonant voice, with all its wisdom and knowledge, creates a sensation among the crowd. Some shout or begin to jerk their bodies. Others break out in uncontrollable laughter and tears of joy. "Surely," one woman exuberantly exclaims, "Ramtha is the voice of Truth speaking to this last-days generation. The New Age is here and we are now God!" Hearing this, a man nearby says simply, "I love Ramtha, I love myself, I love everyone."[1]

Why all the fuss over Ramtha? Who is he? And how can he have such a bizarre and hypnotic effect on average, everyday kind of people like you or me?

Ramtha is an angel—an old angel in a new age. And he is merely one of several kindred spirits who have taken flight recently, claiming to reveal new truths to a new age through human agents called channelers. Ramtha's channeler, for example, is J.Z. Knight, a Seattle mother. Literally, the girl next door. Only this one has become a millionaire through her many public appearances and the sale of thousands of Ramtha video and audio tapes.

People like Mrs. Knight and their human followers refer to their angels variously as their spirit entity, counselor, guide, light-bearer, spiritual friend, internal teacher or advisor. Still others come to know them as their higher self or voice. Others call them ancient or ascended masters, masters of wisdom or the wise ones. But whatever they are called in the New Age, they are by any other name what the Bible calls fallen angels, unclean evil spirits or demons.

> There are only two sources of power that can intelligently operate in thousands of sites around the globe,...communicating directly with hundreds or even thousands of people: God [and his angels] or Satan [and his angels].[2]

And since the communications of Ramtha and Company consistently deny God and reject or distort His Word, we know beyond a doubt with which category many New Age seekers are communing.

Remember God's sorrowful diatribe against the rebellious angel (Isaiah 14:12–13, NKJV)? "How you are fallen from heaven, O Lucifer...for you have said in your heart: 'I will ascend into heaven, I will exalt my throne above the stars of God....'" Pretty outlandish claims, weren't they? Well, in lieu of those, consider these: "I did not die; I ascended!" "In the seed of Lucifer lies God and divineness."[3]

Who does this sound like? You guessed it. It's the chilling, centuries-old echo of Lucifer himself, beating the same old drum through Ramtha and Mrs. Knight in our own twentieth century.

Now a several-thousand-year-old angel speaking through your next-door neighbor might sound just a tad outlandish to you, but to many, Ramtha and a host of other such angels are anything but abnormal. On the contrary, they are a convincing, albeit sensational reaffirmation of an invisible world inhabited by hosts of millions of spirit beings who are the only hope left for mankind. And today, at a time when the human race seems to need help the most, these old angels are generously manifesting like never before and availing mankind with ancient knowledge and wisdom. For many, these old angels hold the secrets to mankind's only hope for this confusing age.

Some of you may be shaking your head, thinking, "You can't be serious!" Others know full well that I am deadly serious because you have seen Mrs. Knight on ABC's "20/20" or "Good Morning America" or the "Phil Donahue Show." And if you have missed Ramtha, then perhaps you heard Sharon Gless of Cagney and Lacey attribute her 1987 Emmy success to her spirit entity "Lazaris."

Probably more than a few of you are among the over 15 million who have read Shirley MacLaine's New Age autobiography *Out on a Limb* inspired by an extraterrestrial angel called the "Mayan." Maybe you have picked up one or more of Jane Roberts' twenty-five books, each inspired by spirit guide "Seth." Or the best-selling *A Course on Miracles* (a book that purports to be Christian, but don't kid yourself) by co-authors Helen Schucman and spirit guide—get this—Jesus!

Then there is Ruth Montgomery and "Lily." Kevin Ryerson and "John." Pat Rodegast and "Emmanuel." Ram Dass and "Emmanuel," Judith Stanton and "Emmanuel." Some of them really get around! The list goes on and on and so does the plethora of books, magazines, tapes, study groups, seminars and retreat centers, which are attracting millions to their teachings. New Age books and literature are almost as ubiquitous as the angels themselves. Angels of the New

Age definitely have landed in every segment of our society. And I mean "every"!

New Age is big business in big business, for example. Over twenty percent of "socially responsible" Fortune 500 companies are investing big dollars to hire therapists, artists and meditation teachers to provide New Age-related training and seminars for their employees.

New Age ideas are also penetrating public education. A friend of mine has three sons—five, seven and nine years of age. One day his youngest came home from nursery school and proudly stuck his freshly colored masterpiece to the fridge door: "My name is Marky. I am a Cancer. My sign is the crab." That same evening, his middle son was working on a paragraph for English on the subject of demons, while the oldest was researching a project on reincarnation, in which, by the way, twenty-five percent of Americans believe.

The entertainment industry has become a major vehicle for the pervasive dissemination of New Age thinking. The arts, of course, is communication. And so the efforts produced by many movie directors, actors, athletes, artists, writers, musicians and singers often reflect and communicate the beliefs of their creators, intentionally or not.

Check your newspaper. Not a week goes by when there is not some kind of community workshop, seminar, class or psychic fair catering to some aspect of the New Age in your area.

What's the big attraction? Just exactly what is the New Age Movement anyway? Why is it growing so rapidly? What do its adherents believe and why do they believe it? And what, if anything, does the recent escalation of interest in angels have to do with it?

Many people question whether a New Age exists at all because the kinds of things in which they believe are really not so "new." It's true. The ideas have been around forever. Still, over the last twenty-five years, there has definitely been a marked and obvious movement away from Western religions and traditional Christianity to Eastern philosophies like Buddhism, Zen, Taoism, Hinduism, ancient mystery religions and the occult.

When I was a kid, missionaries used to show slides of people bowing down to idols in faraway pagan lands. I remember thinking, "How strange!" Not anymore. Today in America, for example, there are an estimated 1.5 million Buddhists. And Islam is one of, if not the fastest growing religions in the world. In England, Hindu and Sikh temples are beginning to outnumber the steeples of that country's ancient Christian cathedrals. As the *New Age Journal* proudly observed recently: "Those who set out today to explore spiritual ideas outside the conventional Judeo-Christian arena may find that what was once a lonely path is now a well-travelled highway."[4]

Another thing that makes the New Age difficult to describe is that it is not a single movement. It is many movements. It is not a single religion. It is many religions. A synergy or cross-fertilization of any number of them. Neither is there a single identifiable leader. There are multiplied thousands of leaders. There is no identifiable constituency with a clearly spelled out and agreed-upon set of beliefs or statement of faith. Rather, it is a loose coalition made up of hundreds of independent, local, self-interest groups. And because each one is so eclectic in nature it is incredibly difficult to pin down or generalize about the movement as a whole. Such an attempt is like trying to gather and organize sparks off a welding torch. There are just too many of them and they are changing all the time.

And yet, there is a strange unity within the diversity. If you take a few reflective steps backward and observe the many sparks, after awhile they really all begin to look the same. And several recurring, dominant and general themes begin to emerge from the apparently diverse streams of thought. After awhile they all seem to be saying sort of the same thing, just in subtly different ways.

Let's identify some of the more prominent unifying sparks or beliefs. When we are done, it will be obvious why old angels are taking our culture by storm.

SATAN, FALLEN ANGELS, EVIL AND HELL

Christians believe in the existence of a very real personal being called Satan who, along with his fallen angels, opposes and hinders God's plan to this day. In contrast, a recurring theme in New Age thought is that there is no personal being called the devil. Satan, demons, hell and evil do not really exist, they say. They are only illusions. There is no evil. Only good or potential good. "Emmanuel," the spirit friend of the authors who compile "his" teaching in *Emmanuel's Book* confirms it:

> *Some of you perhaps are wondering*
> *why I always promise goodness,*
> *why I don't say anything about darkness.*
> *Simply because, from my perspective,*
> *it does not exist.*[5]

"This is the New Age," we are told, "and we need to jettison the old-fashioned biblical and fictional ideas that an evil Satan exists, that a sinful humanity exists and that he and we are somehow personally responsible to a personal God for our own sinfulness. These are outworn concepts—deadweight, antiquated thinking that must be discarded because it is restraining us from discovering our own 'godness' and our own true potential. Abandon the old and join this 'new age movement' away from all of that."

The only problem is, if you deny the existence of a real, personal devil, you also circumvent the necessity for, and therefore the existence of, a real and personal God. After all, if evil does not exist, what need have we for a loving

God who forgives? And so the New Age is all too ready to distort and redefine the biblical presentation of God as well. What have they come up with?

A NEW GOD FOR A NEW AGE?

There is a lot of confusion about who God is today. Have you noticed? Just turn on your radio. One of the most omnipresent songs at the time of this writing is Joan Osborne's "One of Us," successful not only for the mesmerizing melody, but probably even more so for its whimsical lyrics (inane as they are). The songwriter's musings about God include some interesting images that I hadn't thought about lately, like: "What if God was one of us, just a slob like one of us/ Just a stranger on the bus, trying to make his way home?" Hmm. Whatever.

Is that what God is like? In the Crash Test Dummy's 1993 album, "God Shuffled His Feet," and asked people stupid questions like: "Do you have to eat or get your hair cut in heaven/And if your eye got poked off in this life, would it be waiting up in heaven with your wife?" Hmm. Never thought of that one either. Nor the likes of Tori Amos' recent observations: "God, sometimes You don't come through / Do You need a woman to look after you?" Or the cult hit, "Dear God" by Britain's XTC (also recorded by Sara McLachlan), which concludes: "I don't believe in heaven or hell / No pearly gates, no thorny crown / You're always letting us humans down / If there's one thing I don't believe in, it's You." Apparently, neither does Bon Jovi: "Hey God, tell me what the h___ is going on/These days You're even harder to believe." And, oh yes, let's not forget Ramtha. He doesn't sing, but he's never at a loss for words, like, the Christian God is an "idiotic deity."[6]

See what's happening? God is whoever you want Him to be. And everyone, it seems, has some idea, concept or opinion running the gamut from innocent and quizzical to satirical, caustic, angry or downright venomous. In fact, ninety-nine percent of Americans say they believe in some kind of God, albeit their own.

Therefore, the perceptions and descriptions of God are as limitless as those trying to perceive Him. Trying to define the god of the New Age is like trying to package fog. Good luck!

However, fog is still all fog. And regardless of its pervasive density (i.e., diversity of opinions) there are again several common clouds of agreement, even though they are still clouds.

Generally speaking, for example, God is not only "whoever" you want Him to be. He may also be "whatever" you want Him to be. I did a double take at the cover of a book in the religion section recently: What is God? It was no typo. In fact, it is pretty standard for most New Agers to abandon the idea of a personal God with whom one can have a relationship. A depersonalized God still has power, but "It" cannot love, communicate and relate. "It" may be watching us, but as Bette Midler sings: "God is watching us…from a distance." "G_d" (as it is often printed) is impersonal, removed and uninterested. "He," "She" or "It" is more of a cosmic force or power that can be tapped into if you know how. Or "It" is a cosmic consciousness that can be experienced if you develop the ancient wisdom or awareness techniques that reveal such knowledge.

Enter the seminars, workshops, workbooks, journals and weekend retreat centers.

Also, the standard and undergirding New Age philosophy is pantheism. That is to say, "All is God and God is all and all are one." Or, as the Beatles put it in the '60s: "I am he as you are he as you are me and we are all together." All of us and everything else that exists is an expression of the divine oneness of us all. You see the results of a belief in pantheism everywhere, from the overt worship of nature to the subtle, perhaps even ignorant, nuances of it in normal life and people's perception of it.

While skiing recently at a beautiful mountain resort in Canada, I struck up a conversation with an executive officer of the large corporation that owned and operated the ski resort I was enjoying. We got on the topic of God and I asked him who he thought Him to be. Gazing off at the windswept summits of the jagged peaks framing us on the chairlift that day, he gestured reverently with outstretched arms, "This is my god!" Pantheism.

Picking up my clubs at the golf course on the way home from church one Sunday, I received a not unexpected ribbing about my attire (suit and tie).

"What do you expect?" I offered in defense. "I just came from church." Which prompted one fellow to rejoin with a ready and honest response. He raised his putter to the fairways and with full sincerity proudly proclaimed: "This is my god!" Pantheism. He probably didn't even know the word, but the essence of his idea of God was tantamount to my skiing friend who did. Pantheism is any substitute, intentional or inadvertent, for the biblical presentation of God, be it a mountain, a tree, a fairway, golf club or tennis ball. Never were T.S. Eliot's words more appropriate:

> *In the land of lobelias and tennis flannels*
> *The rabbit shall burrow and the*
> *thorn revisit,*
> *The nettle shall flourish on the gravel court,*
> *And the wind shall say: "Here were decent*
> *godless people;*
> *Their only monument the asphalt road*
> *And a thousand lost golf balls."*[7]

YOU'RE LOOKING AT HIM (OR HER)!

Many New Agers believe there is a universal energy or life source in all matter—in this page, in the glasses you are using to read this page, in the rocks and trees outside your window, the bug on your screen, the dust on your ledge.

> *God is everything.*
> *God is in the space between us.*
> *God is in the table in front of you.*
> —PAUL MCCARTNEY

In the movie *The Last Temptation of Christ* Jesus picks up some dust and announces: "This too is my body." Pantheism. In everything is a life source that unites the cosmos. Mother Earth, the sun, the moon, the stars, indeed all of nature can rightfully be worshiped as God. And because a divine universal life force is found everywhere and in everything, then it logically follows that this "godness" is in you and me too.

"The Force dwells within," George Lucas says in *Star Wars*. "You are God," says Ramtha; "God the Father is you."[8] "God's Name is holy, but no holier than yours. To call upon His name is but to call upon your own," writes Helen Schucman in her Course on Miracles. "You are the holy Son of God Himself."[9] "I stand here to remind you that within your own being is the Christ you seek," says Emmanuel.[10]

With no hesitation whatsoever there exists this unabashed belief that all human beings are "god." The only problem is most of us haven't discovered this yet and we need to be enlightened. Therefore, the "great commission" of the New Age is to teach, preach and persuade the world how to become conscious of our own individual "godness." And once that awareness occurs, we will achieve our full and unlimited power and potential. We alone, then, are in charge of our own destiny. The future of mankind, the hope for civilization is solely in our collective hands. Indeed, if all of us could become similarly enlightened, what a wonderful world this would be. A grand global awareness would result in utopia.

Oh, really? Can you imagine a world with 5.8 billion people running around thinking they're god like Shirley MacLaine does? Recently the front page of our local newspaper reported her screaming at some jackhammering construction workers outside her hotel room at three in the afternoon because she couldn't sleep. I guess you can do that if you're god.

Chuckle if you will, but this notion has tremendous appeal to people today. Who doesn't want to be in complete control of his or her own life or even everyone else's for that matter? We all like the sound of that because independence (i.e., pride) is in the heart of all of us. I have yet to meet someone who would not like to think that he or she can somehow contribute to his or her own salvation. To leave everything totally in our own hands resonates with one of the strongest drives in all of us—to answer to no one, to bow to no one, to make and live up to our own set of rules, to be in total control of our own life and destiny. For this reason alone the New Age has potent appeal to many in our increasingly self-reliant and individualistic generation. "Who's God?" they say. "Look in the mirror. You're looking at him (or her)."

Truth, Buffet Style

By now you may be asking, "Where does all this come from? Who is telling, teaching, promising all of this?" A Christian's source of truth is the Bible—a single, inspired volume that has stood the test of time and explains the nature of God, man, the world, angels and all other spiritual truth God intends for us to know. But a single, absolute truth source is unacceptable to a New Ager. "How narrow-minded can you be?" they ask. There are many sources to truth. Pick one. Pick a couple. Make up your own.

And so the smorgasbord of truth options is another source of great appeal to people. You get to choose from a kaleidoscope of very intriguing offerings. For starters, *Ask Your Angels.*" Maybe you are drawn to the teachings of Emmanuel or Seth or Ramtha, for example. For just a small fistful of dollars, buy the books written by those through whom each speaks, and voilá! You have a complete and personal guide to your own inner spirit, the outer world and your ethical decisions and behavior in it.

For a few dollars more, you can regularly consult an astrologer or psychic to order your life. Beware! New Age "truth" sources can get very expensive and addictive. Psychics on late-night television will run you over $5 a minute. Channelers are even more. People pay big dollars to watch channeler Ann Morse trance out to tune in messages from five to six thousand "transeekers" from the Zeta-Reticuli Planet hovering in spacecrafts above the conference room of the Omega Center (a New Age bookstore) in Toronto.[12]

For quite a few dollars more you can receive truth from your very own personal guru or master teacher. If you're a movie or rock star, you can go right to the top. The garden path blazed by the Beatles to the Maharishi Mahesh Yogi in the '60s is now a well-traveled freeway. A recent edition of *Rolling Stone* magazine [13] shows popular rockers from The Beastie Boys, Smashing Pumpkins and the Red Hot Chili Peppers rubbing fraternal shoulders with Buddhist monks and the Dalai Lama.

OK, so you're broke. But anybody can afford to buy a crystal at a garage sale. Apparently you can glean truth from peering into a crystal that holds mystical knowledge and power. Or truth can be revealed as you learn and master a certain practice like biofeedback training, sensory deprivation, progressive relaxation, yoga, meditation or astral projection. Or through contemplative techniques like sensing, listening, intuition, prayer, grounding, releasing, opening, aligning, conversing. Or by understanding and working with your own "chakras" (several energy centers that run from the base of your spine to the top of your head) and the human energy fields.

It's truth, buffet style. Pick one. Pick a couple. Pick your own. Pick mine. Just don't tell anyone yours is the only one and neither will I. It's a buffet, remember. There's more where ours came from and they're all well-founded because you found them. See, the only requirement for yours to be valid is if your own conscience and experience confirm it for you. Your own theology, your life's philosophy flows completely out of your own personal experience. "Always make your heart the final judge," Emmanuel chimes. "Remember, you are God, my dears. Trust that part of you."[14]

WELCOME TO THE MORAL MAZE

Can you imagine what is going to happen to a society based on this kind of ethic, when this kind of relativism is played out in experience to its inevitable, eventual, long-term, logical, egalitarian conclusions? What happens to a society that doesn't distinguish between good and evil, much less even care? Well, for one thing, it is going to have frightening implications for morality.

For example, if you along with thousands of others have chosen, say, Emmanuel to be your truth source, here is what you in good conscience will believe about several contemporary moral issues.

On the topic of divorce, for example, Emmanuel assures you: "If you have joined in union and find that you have grown in different directions, well, hooray for both of you. Be pleased and joyous and move to more compatible surroundings."[15]

On homosexuality: "In the long run, it is a healthy statement in your civilization."[16]

On abortion: "If this act is used for growth, if it opens the way for you to find your own meaning, your own needs, your own truth and beingness, then it is a gift."[17]

Now, how do you argue these things from a biblical position with someone who claims a truth source like this? You don't. They will just come back with, "Mind your own truth source. I'll mind mine." Problem: When you remove one absolute truth source from a society (i.e., the Bible) and replace it with opinion, what you have is a moral maze. There is no basis or authority for ethics, no frame of reference other than the collective conclusions of an imaginative society. Result? A carte blanche recipe for moral chaos, the '60s fulfillment of "anything goes," a crazed, careless and confused generation. Check the news tonight. The telltale results will scream at you.

The thing about a maze is it doesn't come with directions. Just enter and begin groping and feeling your own way through life and hope you eventually arrive safely at some meaninful destination. Basically, the New Age is life without a moral map. James Houston's words ring so true: "To opt for your own godhead leaves you with no recourse to any principles of objective reasoning. It is an ultimate turning inwards upon yourself that leaves out any objective criteria whatever."[18] And, of course, lost in the confusing maze of life.

Well, enter the old angels who are more than ready to help navigate you through the house of mirrors. But where will they take you? Well, how many sparks fly from a welding torch? Beginning to get the picture?

WHERE DO WE ALL END UP?

Other than angels, what is the hottest topic these days? The afterlife. Sherwin Nuland's *How We Die* and Tom Harpur's *Life After Death* at the time of this writing top several secular nonfiction lists. Since its publication in 1992, Betty Eadie's *Embraced by the Light* (about her near-death experience) has sold over 2 million copies. As millions of baby boomers, the largest bulge in our population, en masse round the corner on middle age this decade (an average of 12,000 turn forty everyday in the United States), everyone is thinking about death and dying. And so it should come as no surprise that the New Age offers a win-win solution for your final exit/reincarnation. Almost every New Age philosophy embraces some form of reincarnation (the rebirth of the soul in a new form or body). Eadie herself, drawing on her Mormon faith, talks repeatedly about her "pre-mortal" existence and memory of events and people from her earthly life. Reincarnation.

Emmanuel: "Your ultimate self-realization is
the realization of God, for you and God are
one. This is what you have travelled these
many, many lifetimes to discover."[19]

Wow! Another chance? I don't need to fear death? Apparently not. But what Westerners don't realize (and the New Age won't tell you) is that ours is an altered version of the traditional historic kind of Hindu reincarnation where one can devolve into a lower life form to shed bad karma if one doesn't watch out. You don't hear any of that. It wouldn't wash with the upwardly mobile, progressive urban seeker. No, the reworked reincarnation for North Americans is an optimistic, more palatable "no lose" form, which simply suggests that the more aware you become of your own godness, the more you flow with the life force within you; the more you trust your inner divine energy, the greater likelihood of upward evolvement in your next life until finally you will break free of the cycle of birth and rebirth and you become one with the universe in spirit form once and for all. It's a "win-win" deal. Who's going to argue with that? It's very convenient to believe. Promising. Liberating. Palatable. But is it true?

JESUS WHO?

Helen Schucman: "You are God's Son [Jesus
Christ], one Self, with one Creator and one
goal; to bring awareness of this oneness
to all minds...."[20]

When it comes to Jesus Christ, the most popular New Age notion is that He was simply a good human being upon whom a special concentrated life energy descended called a "God Consciousness." In other words, Jesus was born to a physical father and mother and lived an above-average moral life and that was His unique claim to fame. Jesus is the supreme example of goodness for the rest of us to shoot for. But He is not the only one. Krishna, Buddha, Mohammed, Confucius and others experienced the God Consciousness in their day too. And if you and I were only more enlightened and became more aware of our own godness, the very same God Consciousness could descend on us too.

So who is going to do the enlightening, you might ask?

Enter...Old Angels in a New Age

There is a larger plan at work here. A great
orchestration. The angels are opening up
to us as never before.[21]

Suddenly the heavenly host is upon us, and
in this New Age a grass-roots revolution of the
spirit has people asking all sorts of questions
about angels.[22]

Why all the increased focus on angels today? Once again, Emmanuel:

Your guides are spirits on the plane of forgiveness who have ultimately
forgiven themselves. They now seek to aid you in your own self-forgiveness
and in finding the true Christ within each one of you. My function [is
to]...direct you toward your own inner Light.[23]

Isn't it interesting that people who do not believe in a devil, in evil, in sin nor in a personal God who can forgive that sin, still sense the need for forgiveness? Forgiveness from what, if there is no sin, if evil is an illusion? If we are all god, why do we need forgiveness?

Anyway, assuming we need forgiveness for "something," how can we be forgiven? Well, according to the New Agers we can be forgiven by forgiving ourselves. But that can only happen when we realize we are god and therefore can forgive ourselves because only god can forgive. And who will help guide us to our godness? Who will enlighten us? The authors of *Ask Your Angels* say it can "only happen with the help, guidance and shared wisdom of our angels."[24] See, with God and Satan out of the picture, angels remain mankind's only source and symbol of hope—which explains why angels have taken flight with such gusto in this New Age.

To the New Age seeker, angels appear to be the only supernatural, personal beings or realities left in the universe in whom we can believe, who can point us to salvation. They are our only hope. The terrible, sinister irony is that the hope they offer (fallen as they are) is to point right back to within ourselves in search of good and godness that is just not there, because it is precisely the absence of godness—the emptiness, the despair, the loneliness, pain and sinfulness inside of all of us—that sent us looking for outside help and truth in the first place.

BACK WHERE WE STARTED

See what happens? We are back where we started. It's a circle game. It's ouija. It's yes-yes. It's a lie. And it's hopeless. You can trace it back to where it all began—to the rise and fall of the beautiful angel.

It all sounds so good, so promising. Everyone pick your own track and we'll evolve together to oneness with each other and the universe. But is that really what happens? If you are in the throes of trying to answer some of these concerns, may I suggest an option you may not have considered? Take a close and honest look at the best-selling truth source of all time, the Bible. You will discover that behind all those sparks is a single source of confusion and disparity—that the majority of New Age philosophies are, at the core, based on an old lie by an old angel dressed up for a New Age. Let me explain.

AN OLD LIE BY AN OLD ANGEL

Satan always offers hope. It is a pattern chronicled in great detail throughout Scripture. He's done it from day one, but it has always been false hope. He cannot deliver. Check his track record. He even promised himself hope in Isaiah 14:14: "I will ascend....I will make myself like the Most High." A lie is born. The old angel tells his first one.

What happened next? Ezekiel 28:16 (c.f. Revelation 12:4, 9) tells us that he spread the same lie to one-third of heaven's angels who, for whatever reason, believed it. But instead of becoming gods they were driven in disgrace from the mount of God's heaven. Then, once upon the earth, he and they trafficked the same old lie on humanity. Genesis 3:4-5: "You can be gods too! Come on, trust me" (my paraphrase). And, for whatever reason, they did trust him. But instead of becoming gods, they were driven in disgrace from the paradise of Eden.

A few thousand years later we find the same old angel tempting Jesus. Luke 4:6–7: "All authority has been given to me. I'll share it with you if you worship me. There's room for more than one god around here" (my version). To which Jesus responds: "The buck stops here. There's only one God and you're not He" (my version of verse 8). Foiled again, the devil left Him for easier marks and for the last 2,000 years the old angel has repeated the same old lie in several different and creative ways. Once again the New Age is buying it hook, line and sinker.

Guess what? He's not going to deliver. He never did. He never could. He never will. Because he does not have any hope to deliver! He is the embodiment of hopelessness. There is no possibility for redemption for Satan and his angels and he knows it. His and their fate is sealed. And, as the ages roll on and heaven grows further and further away, Satan moans,

> *Which way I fly is hell; myself am hell.*
> —JOHN MILTON
> *(Paradise Lost)*

However, you and I still have an opportunity to choose not to believe the lie, but to believe the truth as revealed in the Word of God. That hope for mankind does not come from discovering the god in you, but in discovering the opposite: the absence of God in you and the presence of sin. And the only way you will ever get divinity in you is to ask God to remove your sin as only He can and replace it with the cleansing power and presence of His son Jesus Christ. And the God of the universe, the author of the Bible, will take up residence in your heart and you can have a living hope of an inheritance that is undefiled, that cannot fade away and is reserved in heaven for you (1 Peter 1:3-4). I don't know about you, but that reasonates with me! It can for you too if you choose the same road.

PICK A ROAD, ANY ROAD?

> There is a way [road] that seems
> right to a man,
> but in the end it leads to death.
> (Solomon in Proverbs 14:12)

I was watching *Alice in Wonderland* with my daughter. She got all excited at one point and began telegraphing Alice's next encounter by chanting: "Pink cat, Daddy! Pink cat!" Sure enough, a couple of scenes later, Alice comes to a fork in the road and asks the pink cat for advice. The conversation goes something like this:

> *"Cheshire Puss, would you please tell me which way I ought to go from here?"* queried a lost and confused Alice.
> *"Well, that depends a good deal on where you want to get to,"* replied the cat.
> *"I don't much care where,"* Alice responded.
> *"Well, then it doesn't much matter which way you go,"* said the cat.

In other words, Alice, "Pick a road, any road."

Many people today (maybe even you) are like poor Alice—desperately looking for some sort of direction in life, but just not knowing which road to take. There are so many options. And they all look so good. There are many roads to God or godness, we are told, and many ways and means to relate to Him. And each is "right in its own way" but none is right if it declares itself the only way. How does anyone, I ask, know anymore which road will lead them through the confusing maze of life to some sort of meaningful navigation and conclusion?

According to the New Age, the test for knowing God and finding meaning in life and death is multiple choice. Choose A, B, C, D or E (all of the above). You can't go wrong because there is no right and wrong answer. Emmanuel: "To believe in the God in everyone is the ultimate religion. It does not matter what path you take to get there."[25]

By contrast, consider the words of Jesus Christ, the true Emmanuel from Matthew 7:13–14: "Enter through the narrow gate. For wide is the gate and broad is the road that leads to destruction, and many enter through it. But small is the gate and narrow the road that leads to life, and only a few find it."

According to the Bible, the test for knowing God and finding meaning in life and death is not multiple choice. There is only one correct answer and it is based on the objective facts of Scripture, not subjective feelings of the masses.

Throughout history God has provided a way or path that leads to Himself. In fact, the Bible is really a road map through the maze of life. It contains reliable instructions for finding God and ultimate meaning in life. And although the road that leads you there may very well be narrow, even difficult, it does lead to eternal rest, life and reward. So, is it E (all the above)? No. There is only one answer. Only one way. Jesus says, "I am the way [road] and the truth and the life. No one comes to the Father except through me" (John 14:6).

Jesus says the only way to God is through Him, period. The New Age says the only way to God is through "all of the above," comma. It can't be both. One of them is lying. Who are you going to believe?

To every man there openeth
A Way, and Ways and a Way.
And the High Soul gropes the High Way,
And the Low Soul gropes the Low,
And in between, on the misty flats,
The rest drift to and fro.

But in the end there openeth
A High Way, and a Low,
And every man decideth
The Way his soul should go.

—JOHN OXENHAM
("The Ways")[26]

Entertaining Angels

"Come to the edge," he said.
They said, "We are afraid."
"Come to the edge," he said.
They came.
He pushed them...and they flew."

—GUILLAUME APOLLINAIRE

VERYBODY NEEDS "a little angel shove" now and then, don't they? Every year when Christmas arrives at our church campus we play a little game between our school and church staffs called "Angels and Earthlings." A few weeks before Christmas several "angels" randomly draw the name of their "earthling" out of a hat. Then for the next several days leading up to Christmas, the angels anonymously minister to their earthlings with little gifts, words of encouragement and the like. Before the break for the holidays, in one final visible angel shove, these terrestrial celestials reveal themselves to their earthlings and wish them a Merry Christmas.

You know, "angels and earthlings" is based on good theology. Hebrews 13:2 says, "Be not forgetful to entertain strangers: for thereby some have entertained angels unawares" (KJV). In other words, "Be an angel yourself!"

We have already learned that sometimes for the purposes of God, angels can and do materialize to entertain or render service to human beings. Now it appears that sometimes for the purposes of God, angels materialize to be entertained or to receive service from human beings of all things. The point should be well taken. After all, how would you treat a person if you knew on the off chance he or she might be a messenger from God—an angel? That is what the verse is saying. Kind of gives new meaning to the Golden Rule, doesn't it?

You might ask, how does one "entertain," "minister to" or "treat" an angel? The best place to get an answer is to look at how angels "entertain" us, how angelic spirits minister to earthlings, then go and "do unto angels as you would have angels do unto you."

So, what do "angels do unto you"? That was the subject of the third and fourth chapters where we looked at a day in the life of one—an angel's job description. Consider the elements of that in light of this and something very interesting emerges: Almost everything holy angels are busy zipping about doing for earthlings in a supernatural way, earthlings are capable of doing for one another in natural ways.

Who among us, for example, like an angel, is not able to render service, strengthen, encourage or comfort another human being in need, stress, danger, distress or turmoil, be it physical, emotional or spiritual? All of us are equipped to express or demonstrate compassion at relative levels to various people at diverse and sundry times.

Or, do you think you are capable of assisting, protecting, defending or delivering someone in trial or trouble or indecision or despair or disaster? Of course you are—in many different ways.

What about praying? Can we be active in offering prayer to God as the angels are active in answering prayer for Him? Can we worship God from earth like angels are known to do in heaven on a daily basis? Some angels, that is all they do—worship God all day long. So can we. In fact, for the follower of Jesus, all of life should be an act of worship—a daily outpouring of service and worship as a love offering to God (Romans 12:1–2).

There is more.

Who among us cannot reach out and touch someone lonely, ill or near death? We can all be agents of Christ's grace, mercy and love to the hurting, the dying, the homeless. We can all stop to at least acknowledge, touch or give to a suffering person in obvious need. Or, depending on the situation, like the angels in the early chapters of the Gospels, be an agent of God's message of hope and deliverance by forewarning others or announcing encouragement or heralding the good news of Jesus Christ to a hopelessly lost and spiritually seeking world. These are all the things angels do for us and as such give us a pretty good indication of what is expected from us.

You might be interested to know that the word "angel" that you read in your English Bible is transliterated from the Hebrew word *mal'ak* in the Old Testament and the Greek *angelos* in the New Testament (as in Los Angeles, City of Angels). Both words mean "messenger" and are used to describe anyone who has a "message-bearing role" be they human being or spirit being. Yes, even human beings can be "angels" (1 Kings 19:2; Luke 7:24; 9:52). Only the context determines whether a *mal'ak* or *angelos* is heavenly (Matthew 24:36) or human. The only difference in *angelos* is that some are spirits and some are people. But both are called to render service in similar ways.

Saint Augustine clarified this nicely several hundred years ago:

Angels are spirits, but it is not because they are spirits that they are angels. They become angels when they are sent. For the name angel refers to their office, not their nature. You ask the name of its nature, it is spirit; you ask its office, it is that of an angel, which is a messenger.[1]

Conversely, with all due respect to Augustine (who I'm sure would not mind me synchronizing my thoughts with his), can the same be said of earthlings?

> *Earthlings are angels too, but it is not because they are humans that they are angels. They become angels when they, too, are sent. For the name angel refers to their office, not their nature. You ask the name of an earthling's nature, it is human being; you ask its office, it is that of an angel, which is a messenger...a voice for God.*

There are invisible spirit messengers or holy "angels" all around you right now. They number in the billions, each one of them fearfully and wonderfully and uniquely created by God and each one faithfully serving Him by serving us. But there are also several other visible, potential "people angels" surrounding you in your little corner of the universe at this moment too. Perhaps a spouse is close by. Does your husband, for example, look like an angel? Maybe that is not dandruff on his shoulder after all. Maybe it is angel dust.

Does your wife resemble an angel? A friend of mine said his wife was a real angel. When I asked why, he replied, "because she's always up in the air harping that she has nothing to wear!"

What about your children? Little angels (like mine!)? One mother was putting her little boy to bed one night. He was fearful of the dark and so she asked God to surround his bed with guardian angels to protect him. Although she sensed that he was not entirely convinced, it seemed to provide him an element of reassurance.

"Mommy," sighed the lad as his mother got up to leave, "thanks for praying for the angels. But what I really need tonight is somebody with skin on!"

He needed an *angelos* that he could see, touch and feel. And Mommy's skin seemed to fit the bill more than some invisible feathers that particular night. Well, that is the essence of our teaching in these pages. Can we be angels with skin on? We can. Indeed, we must. In the year 1850, Henry Wadsworth Longfellow wrote:

We have not wings, we cannot soar;
But we have feet to scale and climb
By slow degrees, by more and more,
The cloudy summits of our time.[3]

(*The Ladder of St. Augustine*)

"We have not wings, we cannot soar." We are not that kind of angel, nor will we ever be. But we can still be angelic or angel-like to one another on the off chance that we are rubbing shoulders with an angel or Jesus or another human being, all of whom are worthy of the same treatment, wouldn't you agree? Here, then, let me give you a little angel shove!

Do not forget to entertain strangers, for by so doing some people have entertained angels without knowing it. (Hebrews 13:2)

This to me is the most curious, fascinating and mysterious verse in the whole Bible. It has always intrigued me. It has at once motivated and encouraged me and yet haunted me ever since several related and eventful experiences riveted home its meaning and changed the life of my wife and me forever.

I don't know how this verse will work its way out in your life, but I hope it does. And I hope the stories in this chapter and the next will somehow be a catalyst for that as I relate to you how it came alive for us. But I want to tell you up front that I tell it with some hesitation.

Spiritual experiences are intensely personal, and as such they find their safest home couched in the privacy of one's own reflections. I think of Mary (the mother of Jesus) in this regard. She had several spiritual encounters in her young life, but chose not to say anything. Instead, "Mary treasured up all these things and pondered them in her heart" (Luke 2:19). I love that image. Some things are just too private to disclose. Too personal to reveal. Too intimate to share. After all, who is going to believe me? Best just to digest them thoroughly, thoughtfully and privately in my own heart.

Many of the people who have contributed stories to this book understand this sentiment as well. We would just as soon ponder them rather than publish them. Encounters with angels are spiritually defining moments. They change you. You know what you experienced and no one in the world will ever persuade you that you imagined it. But why take the chance? It's much safer to digest them in the privacy of our own journals, musings and the odd "safe" conversation.

On the other hand, Mary's very personal ponderings somehow made their way into the world's best-selling book for all to see, didn't they? At least once a year at Christmas for the last 2,000 years, millions worldwide read and sing about them over and over again. The result? Every time we hear them our own hearts are warmed and encouraged. We are changed and blessed by entering into her experiences. It is with that kind of spirit that I proceed—that you might be similarly changed by entering into ours. If that occurs, then I suspect that is partially why they happened to us in the first place.

An Angel on the Line?

One night not long ago I was lying in bed fast asleep. I thought I heard the phone ring as you always do for the first couple of rings during a sound sleep. That was quickly confirmed when my wife gave me the dreaded tap on the shoulder.

"Wake up. There's someone on the phone who wants to talk to a pastor."

I reluctantly but dutifully took the phone and listened to a woman explain how a troubled, hurting individual had called her establishment for encouragement (she thought) or at least a listening ear. She was not sure exactly how, but thought I could help because she could not.

I was not quite awake and to my own shame neither was I impressed. I am afraid I probably communicated that to the caller. Several minutes passed while I quizzed her further; then finally and begrudgingly gave her permission to relay my number to the waiting person. I hung up, sat down on the couch and waited for the phone to ring. It never did. I suspect that somewhere in the process of the previous several minutes the person had interpreted the delayed response as rejection and had given up.

I was now wide awake and realized what had happened. I went to bed a very sad man. Hebrews 13:2 had come to haunt me again. Nestled in my pillow, I had only one question burning into my conscience, which I directed to my wife: "What if that person was an angel, Karen?"

"Exactly what I was thinking," she replied, knowing precisely what I meant.

I prayed: "Lord, forgive me for leaving an angel out in the cold. For ignoring You. For letting You down. If ever I see a person in need again, help me to see Your face or that of an angel."

As I lay there, these thoughts triggered the VCR of my mind to replay a series of separate but intimately related events that occured in staccato fashion over a three-week period in 1988, events that would forever change our attitude toward angels and our perceptions about people in general.

ENTERTAINING ANGELS?

It all began one night, oddly enough, in Texas. We owned a men's clothing store in Canada at the time and were in Dallas for a sportswear trade show. We were excited about a solid week of a little business and a lot of fun, which would include a Washington-Dallas football game. We also planned to spend some time with friends who were attending Dallas Theological Seminary.

One night while they were showing us around town, they asked if we wanted to see where the Dallas Mavericks played their NBA basketball games. Well, I could not get there fast enough. Maybe on the off chance there would be a game and we could slip in for a few hoops! Add that to an NFL game and our trip would be complete! Karen was not quite so anxious, but following some tense negotiations, agreed that an afternoon at the Galleria Shopping Center would be a pretty fair exchange.

We parked a couple of blocks from the arena and excitedly proceeded down a dark street in its direction. Now, I do not know about you, but big cities scare me at night. However, we were with the pros, so not to worry. Suddenly, two figures, a man and a woman, literally materialized out of nowhere and confronted us. They looked like human scarecrows, dressed in rags, dark, dirty skin, almost impish looking. They were obviously very, very poor. I remember them looking like they were hastily and poorly dressed and made up for a drama or impromptu skit. Their pathetic appearances were almost too convincing to be authentic—that is how bad, how sad, how desperate they looked.

The "husband" did the talking and began spinning a tale about living under the bridge and having no money to feed their six children. I remember thinking, "Yeah, right," and to my own embarrassment felt a certain suburban revulsion toward them and anger for their untimely intrusion on our evening. And I suppose if they had approached me instead of my friend I would have acted on this initial reaction and dismissed them with disdain or fear or both.

But instead they addressed him, sensing him somehow to be either the authority or mercy figure in our little group. I watched, wondering how he was going to respond. And he did an amazing thing. He pulled a $5 bill out of his pocket. I thought, *Surely he's not going to give them money!* He displayed the bill, then calmy said, "I want to give you this, but first, I want you to listen to me. You have given me the chance to tell you something that is very important to me and I think it is important for you as well. You need this money, but you need to be loved too."

Then he proceeded to tell them just how much God loved them and how He sent His Son into the world so that whoever believed in Him would have everlasting life. As he proceeded, a calm seemed to descend on us all. Our fears began to dissipate. My revulsion was replaced with sympathy and genuine sorrow. I think I even saw a faint smile crease the man's shadowed lips as our friend finished and then extended his hand with the gift. They took the money and vanished.

I remember thinking firstly, *Where did our friend get the nerve to do that?* Then, secondly, *Who were these people?*

Well, who were they? Were they angels? Maybe. Maybe not. Strangers? Definitely strangers. What did that verse say again? "Do not neglect to show hospitality to strangers, for by this some have entertained angels without knowing it" (NAS).

It did not dawn on me that night that we may very well have been harbingers of hospitality and good news to a couple of angels. Not until we returned to our own town and a second, even more telltale incident quickly occurred did the significance of it all grip me. I immediately journaled the details.

Sometimes things happen in life that unless documented quickly hasten from the fact files of our brain to the imagination section. And it is not long before time steals the details and all that remains is a vague or faint or even phantom recollection of an event that years later we ourselves begin to question ever really happened. From the effervescent glow on the face of the person relaying this episode I knew this was one of those. I did not want time to claim this one, so I wrote it down in story form exactly how it happened.

A Lady and a Stranger

Thump-thump. Thump-thump. A large, soiled mitten timidly rapped on the window of a parked car. The lone occupant squinted through the frosted glass and rudely gestured the man to go away. "Go thump on somebody else's window, ya bum! Street people!" he muttered contemptuously under his middle-class breath.

An expectant glint quickly faded from the hollow, whiskered face. Dejected, he turned away. And, revolving slowly on tired old legs, he retreated a few steps, out of the exposing glare of the mall's bright lights back into the safety of a narrow string of shadows, which extended from the legs of the large billboard that lit up the mall's entrance.

He huddled there, motionless, in a small but clouded niche of secure darkness, meditating on his misfortune. Reflecting the bright neon from the overhanging sign, large white, electric flakes of snow glittered downward, destined for earth, some instead disappearing into the shadow and dying on the hood and shoulders of a heavy gray overcoat.

He stood there, mannequin-like, for several minutes. Then stepped forward to another car that had just pulled up. Another pathetic attempt met with similar results and the old man's heart despaired.

He meant no offense. Just a few dollars to fill the emptiness in his stomach. Was that too much to ask? Especially at Christmas. Some acknowledgment. A smile to warm a cold heart. "Ah, what's the use." Life had long since forsaken such social niceties and seasonal gratuities, and he was used to it—sort of. He really didn't expect anything.

But, again, a braver notion overtook him. "Perhaps the Instant Teller will produce better fortune." With renewed hope he caught the closing door and slipped in out of the cold. He removed the tattered mittens and pushed them into the deep pocket of his long overcoat. Stamping the sticky snow from his rubber boots, he ran a gnarled finger across a runny nose and began to sniffle annoyingly.

She had watched the whole pitiful pantomime from the front seat of her warm car and despair too tugged at her heart. For she loved the rejected. Her heart broke for the heartbroken. She was a woman now, but her heart was still as soft as a child's.

Swallowing back a salty tear, the lady hastened to the Instant Teller door. Slipping her entrance card from the slot, she brushed past the vagrant and several other harried, impatient patrons and took her place last in a long line.

A nervous backward glance revealed the still-huddled figure of the expectant intruder. She snapped her head back but the image was now indelibly etched in her mind like when you mistakenly glance at a light bulb and your eyes take a picture of it. Open or closed, the image wouldn't go away.

The lineup dwindled and they were now alone. She hadn't looked back again but she knew he remained. Heavy, tired breaths heaved from the weary statue. A soft squishing came from his rubber boots as he shifted nervously in the puddle of melted snow in which he now stood.

The machine spat out five, fresh twenty-dollar bills and the lady slipped four of them into her eelskin purse. Pivoting cautiously, she carefully walked toward the old man and, facing him, stopped. Rigid with fear, she stiffened—and waited.

He raised his head. Their eyes met. She saw a lifetime of disappointment etched in that face. It was a tired face, a hungry face, a face drained of hope. His hollow cheeks were blanched pale and creamy-white like old snow. The milky, translucent skin looked as if it would dint like putty if you touched it. Thick, bushy eyebrows drooped lazily, barely revealing the empty glare of cloudy blue eyes, glazed glassy-gray like an old poodle's.

It was a tired, gaunt face. But it was a kind face. The laughter had long since died on those chapped and cracking lips, but a radiant charm had somehow been seasoned into it all. And that's what she saw, quickly erasing her initial fear. In place, a spring of love gushed from her heart and she felt safe.

Pushing a new $20 bill into the crooked yellow hand, she broke the silence:

"Please sir, the $20. Don't buy a bottle with it, promise? Spend it on a hot meal. You look so tired, so hungry."

Another wave of trepidation momentarily surged as she anticipated an unknown response. Admonishing herself for adding the silly, stereotypical rider about the bottle, she dreaded what would happen next. But, oh, how she loved the old man.

A lengthy silence followed, broken only by the crackling of the new bill as his fist clenched and squeezed nervously around it.

She continued speaking with words strangely not her own, sensing only the emergent and irresistible urge to encourage, to love and to deliver good news to this stranger.

"Did you know God loves you?" A silent, but purposeful nod seemed to confirm the query at least enough to energize her to continue.

"...and that if you asked Him to be your Savior, He would. And if you died tonight, you'd go straight to heaven."

As quickly as those words sprung from her mouth she wondered where they had come from. They had the odd, haunting echo of ones spoken by someone else in Dallas just a week before. Somehow they didn't even sound just right to her. But somehow he understood, she felt. Something barely confident restored within her as the man raised his head and cleared his throat. Then in a dull, lifeless monotone, he mumbled:

"Can I say something?"

"Y-yes. Please do," she stammered hopefully.

"Dear Jesus," he began. And shy as a child, he dropped his head and awkwardly began to pray: "Thank You for this gracious lady. I don't know nothing and I never done nothing right. But I know love when I see it and this gracious lady cares. Thank You, Jesus, for this lady."

Her heart strangely warmed. The man was no threat. She continued boldy for, oddly enough, they were still alone.

"Oh, sir, you do know God loves you, don't you? Would you like to ask Jesus to be your Savior right now?"

"Yes, madam. I'd like that." Her head pounded anxiously.

"Pray with me." A gray-haired, homeless old man and a pretty blond suburban woman bowed tandem heads in a hushed and temporary sanctuary in a most unlikely spot on the globe.

"Dear Jesus," she began.

"Dear Jesus," he repeated.

"I am a sinner; I need You."

"I am a sinner; I need You."

"Forgive me."

"Forgive me."

"Come into my heart."

"Come into my heart."

"And make me whiter than snow. Amen."

"And make me whiter than snow. Amen."

"God bless you, sir."

"God bless you, gracious lady."

Pulling the wet hood over his matted head the man tugged his mittens from the one large pocket. He shed a simple but radiant smile, turned, pushed the door open and stepped out onto the icy sidewalk. The lady's watery eyes tenderly tracked each step as the fragile figure slowly inched away.

The bright headlights of a car pulling up outside startled her from a trancelike state. And then another car. And another. "Interesting," she mused. "Here come the people again." It was her signal to leave and she too entered the night only to catch the vanishing silhouette of the stranger blend into the shadows as the cold and darkness swallowed him up.

Checking her watch, the lady quickly sped off in her warm car. Her husband was arriving home soon from work and they had plans for a festive supper and evening out with friends.

An angel? Try and tell my wife he wasn't. And the stranger? She never saw him again. But Karen has never been the same. She is convinced he was an angel. Recently, as she was flipping through my Bible, she said, "Look!" There in the margin beside Matthew 25:35–40 were these words: "Karen's angel, December, 1988." They marked the following interesting exchange between Jesus and some people:

> *Jesus:* For I was hungry and you gave me something to eat, I was thirsty and you gave me something to drink, I was a stranger and you invited me in, I needed clothes and you clothed me, I was sick and you looked after me, I was in prison and you came to visit me.
>
> *People:* Lord, when did we see you hungry and feed you, or thirsty and give you something to drink? When did we see you a stranger and invite you in, or needing clothes and clothe you? When did we see you sick or in prison and go visit you?
>
> *Jesus:* I tell you the truth, whatever you did for one of the least of these brothers of mine, you did for me.

It is time to update our verse (Hebrews 12:3, my version) a bit: "Don't forget to entertain strangers, for some who have done this have entertained Jesus without knowing it. When you were serving them, you were serving Me in disguise." Wow!

ENTERTAINING JESUS?

Francis of Assisi was terrified of leprosy. One day, right in the middle of a narrow path he was travelling, he encountered a leper. Instinctively his heart shrank back, recoiling from the contamination of that loathsome disease. But then he rallied and, ashamed of himself, ran and cast his arms around the sufferer's neck, kissed him and blessed him. Then he passed on. A moment later he looked back. No one was there. For the rest of his life, Francis was certain it was not a leper at all, but Christ Himself whom he had met.

Someone once said to Mother Teresa, "I wouldn't touch a leper for $10,000."

Neither would I," she replied, "but I would willingly tend him for the love of God."

Now, that is a heartbeat of heaven. What would happen to this world if everybody's heart beat like that for everybody else? If each one of us treated the other like we would treat an angel or Jesus Himself?

RECAP: Everybody needs a little angel shove now and then. Look outside yourself today, this week, for a likely prospect (they're easy to spot) and be an angel, will you? Be kind. Everyone you meet today is fighting a battle. Everyone.

Resolve this moment to put some shoe leather to this 2,000-year-old challenge from the apostle Paul (Romans 12:16–21, *The Message*):

Make friends with nobodies; don't be the great somebody...
discover beauty in everyone...

Our Scriptures tell us that if you see your enemy hungry, go buy that person lunch, or if he's thirsty, get him a drink. Your generosity will surprise him with goodness. Don't let evil get the best of you; get the best of evil by doing good.

Give a little angel shove.

Be an "Angel"!

WAS WALKING through a mall last Christmas when a sign promoting a local charity caught my eye. The caption read: "Be an Angel!" Whether the advertisers knew it or not, it made good sound sense.

No, we are not to be angels in the spirit-being sense nor will we ever become that kind of angel. I am not suggesting that we do or be something or someone supernatural—a "friend from high places." But we can be a friend to our own towns, cities, neighborhoods, families. We can be angels or messengers to them.

The first jogger who ran with the news of Greek victory from Marathon to Athens was an "angel" to the Greeks and the news he delivered was the *evangel*. In fact, the words "good news" (from which we get "gospel") in the Bible come from the Greek *euangelion*.

We can all be messengers of heaven (evangelists, if you will), harbingers of God's love, heralds of peace, agents of grace, message bearers to other people. Indeed, you may be the only "angel" some person will ever see. Maybe you do not have wings. Maybe you cannot soar. But you have feet to scale and climb, don't you? And in your own clumsy, earthbound, stumbling fashion you can in some sense fly with the angels of heaven. There is always someone out there who needs some good news, who needs a little angel shove.

According to studies, most of us would like to do a little "shoving." Within most people there flickers a spark of mercy, pathos and philanthropy just waiting to be fanned into a productive flame. A recent report entitled "Fears and Fantasies of the American Consumer" revealed that three out of four of us have daydreamed about saving someone's life and one out of three have dreamed about finding a cure for cancer. Sadly, though, when asked about our greatest pleasure in life, watching television topped the list. Another survey (the Elkos study on "Rethinking Government," 1995) said that Canadians confess that compassion increasingly takes a backseat in our politics of self-interest. It seems we all know the rewards (to both giver and receiver) of reaching out, but we tend to live within ourselves instead.

Psychiatrist Dr. Karl Menninger was once asked, "What would you advise someone to do if he felt a nervous breakdown coming on?" By this point, his answer shouldn't surprise you: "Lock up your house, go across the railroad tracks, find someone in need, and do something to help that person."

Be an angel.

> *While there is a lower class, I am in it; while*
> *there is a criminal element, I am of it; while*
> *there is a soul in prison, I am not free.*

ENTERTAINING ANGELS, CONTINUED

Well, our experiential exegesis of Hebrews 13:2 was not over yet. It was my turn to discover what being an angel meant for me.

The week after Karen's encounter at the bank, things returned pretty well back to normal. It was the Christmas season and my clothing store was very busy. Late one hectic Friday afternoon I finally forced myself away from the cash register and ran over to the adjacent mall to grab a quick lunch. I assured my assistants that I would be right back.

I waded through the sea of shoppers, literally bouncing and bobbing my way to my favorite fast-food outlet and ordered up their health food special: chili dog and fries (extra grease) and a carbonated soda. Any reader in the retail business will relate to a mall diet like this.

It was an exciting time for me. I love Christmas. I especially loved working in the store during the festive season. I would crank up the Lee Greenwood Christmas tape and sell! So I was very pumped as I waited impatiently for my gourmet meal to come so I could get back and sell some more!

Carols were blaring over the mall's sound system too and bag-toting shoppers were madly bustling about. As I was waiting and scanning the surroundings I noticed a huddled figure, vaguely familiar, sitting on a bench. His head was lowered. He was obviously very sad. He did not seem to fit the holiday scenario. All this gaiety and by cruel contrast this scene of obvious pathos. It did not seem right. It left me unsettled.

I knew the man. He had been in my store. Just a couple of times. We had shot the breeze—the general breeze at that, which in itself, come to think of it, was kind of odd. He was obviously poor. I never thought of him as a potential customer and I never tried to sell him anything for fear I would embarrass him, knowing he could never afford even the least expensive item in the store. So why would he stop by like he did?

I struck up a time-filler conversation with him, which immediately confirmed my sense of his deep despondency. *But really*, I thought, *this is not my problem. A lot of people are depressed at Christmastime.* I had a store full of potential customers who were not or at least did not appear to be. And if they were, at least they had money to help spend some of their depression away. I was more than happy to help with that kind of depression.

I grabbed my lunch, bid the man good-bye and headed back to my store. But not without an uncomfortable sense of anxiety dogging my heels with every retreating step until about halfway back when it literally reached out and lurched me to a screeching halt. I heard a voice, not audible, but a voice nevertheless. I cannot describe it to you other than to say it was at once internal, yet other-worldly. Perhaps it was more of a nudging—an angel shove! Yes, that's what it was.

"Go back!"

I argued (in my mind of course). "The store is full of customers! I'm already late! My chili dog will get cold. There's nothing worse than a cold chili dog. A hot one is bad enough!"

"Go back."

It was then that I noticed that the screen of my mind had been replaying the events of the last two weeks and I sensed they were somehow telegraphing a similar destiny for me. I spun on my heels and ran back, breathing a sigh of relief to find the slouching figure still there, head lowered, just like I had left him.

I sat down beside him. He looked up, relieved, yet somehow almost as if he had expected my return. I put my hand on his shoulder.

"How ya doin'?" Tears. Then, to my own shock, I started talking to him about Jesus. I do not remember what I said or how I said it or even why. But I remember the feeling. I remember sensing some latent, familiar, internal support and encouragement gleaned from certain vivid recollections of similar events not far removed.

I recall few details of our dialogue, but five minutes later we were bowing our heads together in the busiest part of the mall. He prayed to ask Jesus Christ into his life. The hand of another beggar reached out to the hand of the King. And the angels of heaven cancelled choir practice to party over the most recent addition to God's family.

We opened our eyes and a small fellow I could only describe as "cute" had obviously been watching the whole affair.

"Praise the Lord! That was beautiful. I am a believer too!" he said. We three talked for a while, then I bid farewell, leaving invitations for them to come by the store sometime to chat. Both smiled and agreed. But do you know what? I never saw either again.

Angels? Maybe. Maybe not. If they were, then how do you explain their ready response to God's offer of eternal life if angels don't understand it or can't receive it (1 Peter 1:12)? I can't. Was God giving some overly curious ones a chance to at least look into it? Perhaps, but not likely. Was God testing our reaction or response to the needs of others? Could be. Were they sent for our benefit and not theirs at all? It did change our lives and revolutionize our faith. Or were they human *angel*oi whom God placed masterfully, like a piece of a puzzle, into our lives for our and their benefit? I'm afraid these ones are going on my "wait until I get to heaven to ask" list with a whole bunch of other ones.

But for now, well, you may never believe that "our" strangers were angels. I'm not asking you to. But you will never convince us they were not. Anyway, that's really not the point, is it? The point is, even if they were not, they were needy strangers and as such may have been angels unawares or Jesus Himself, thereby warranting the heartbeat of heaven.

ONE MORE, JUST FOR GOOD MEASURE

A couple of months passed. And just as these special memories began to fade, God added a very appropriate caveat to our trilogy—a fitting epilogue to seal them forever.

After church one Sunday my wife and I stopped by the instant bank teller to get money for lunch. As I waited outside (Karen does the banking, as you have probably realized by now), I watched an old man, a street person, rustle through a garbage can and then shuffle off down the street. I tracked him in the rearview mirror and, feeling sorry for him, wondered if I should do something.

Just then Karen exited the instant teller. She too noticed the man. Then I watched as my lady, high heels and all, ran half a city block to grab the sleeve of an old gray overcoat and stuff something into a gnarled but grateful old hand. Moments later, out of breath, she climbed into the comfort of our warm car, slumped back in the seat and turned her face toward me. A tear in her eye met with a tear in mine. Neither said a word. We each knew what the other was thinking: "Do not forget to entertain strangers, for by so doing some people have entertained angels without knowing it."

Can you think of anyone who needs a little angel shove? Open your eyes. They are all around you. The poor. The discarded. The prisoner. The sick. The grieving. The abandoned. The divorced. The widowed. The elderly. The infirm. The bedridden. The lonely. The point is, you do not have to look under a bridge or in a crowded mall or outside an instant teller. Maybe you need only to look as close as under your own roof. Who have you been ignoring lately? A son or daughter who is crying out to you for attention? A wife or husband? An aging parent? A neighbor? A student? An employee?

Listen, you don't have to pack your bags like Patrick Swayze did in a Hollywood movie (*City of Joy*) and head off to India to find the pathetic and the poor. In fact, Mother Teresa, whom we all admire for doing just that in real life, surprisingly tells the rest of us not to:

I know you think you should make a trip to Calcutta, but I strongly advise you to save your airfare and spend it on the poor in your own country. It's easy to love people far away. It's not always easy to love those who live right next to us. There are thousands of people dying for a piece of bread, but there are thousands more dying for a bit of love or a bit of acknowledgement.

The truth is that the worst disease today is not leprosy or tuberculosis;

it's being unwanted. It's being left out. It's being forgotten or ignored. The greatest scourge is to be so suffocated with things that we forget the next person.

The "next person" just might be…well, by now you get the point. What a tragedy, if given the chance, to miss the opportunity to entertain angels unawares, to allow our own preoccupations, self-absorption and business to anesthetize us to the needs of others, to leave us mysteriously disappointed with ourselves and our own sad lack of sensitivity and inaction. What a tragedy!

Lord, open my eyes that I may see,
Strangers who need a touch from Thee.
Angels disguised and beckoning me,
To impart Christ's love impartially.

SOME ANGEL TIPS

A common theme in angel stories is vagrants, the homeless and the poor—people who naturally evoke our sympathy and assistance. Recent estimates indicate at least 3 million people in the United States alone are homeless. That's roughly one out of every 100 citizens living on the streets or in shelters.

A few years ago, Canadian Press ran a piece called "Kindness best policy if beggars approach." It included the following helpful advice on what to do if you are approached by someone asking for money. The ideas are from Canadian and American organizations that help the homeless and the poor. Although the suggestions are crafted for them, many of the principles apply to any one of us at some time or another. Indeed, as already stated, everyone you meet is fighting a battle at some relative level on a daily basis and as such is a candidate for a caring touch—an angel shove.

Do:

1. Give, if you have the inclination and the money.

2. Even if you can't or don't want to give, stop and acknowledge the person asking. Look at them. Wish them luck or God's blessing.

3. Stop and talk for a few minutes if you have time. For many, it will be their only human contact that day.

4. Buy whoever is asking a cup of coffee, a sandwich or a meal.

5. Ask local officials why there are so many homeless or panhandlers in your neighborhood. Are there enough services to help? How can you help?

6. Make a donation to a food bank or a service organization if you don't want to give to an individual.

7. Get involved. Volunteer at a food bank or shelter.

8. Touch them.

Do Not:

1. Brush by people asking for your help as if they do not exist or are inhuman.

2. Tell whoever is asking to "Get a job!" or "Get a life!"

3. Worry about what that person is going to do with the money you give. Once it leaves your hand it is a gift. And a gift expects no returns.

Panhandling is an act of desperation. It is an act of survival. (Fred Karnas, National Coalition for the Homeless, Washington)

Even if you don't have any money or aren't inclined to give, it's important to look a person in the eye and speak to them...just to recognize that there's a human being in front of you who's worthy of recognition. (Cliff Newman, Community for Creative Non-Violence, Washington)

Every one of these people is someone's father, son, brother, sister or mother. There but for the grace of God go any of us. (Derek Steeney, Daily Bread Food Bank, Toronto)

He who is kind to the poor lends to the LORD, and he will reward him for what he has done. (Solomon, Proverbs 19:17)

Etched on a church wall in England are the following words:

I will not wish thee riches nor the glow of greatness, but that wherever thou dost go some weary heart shall gladden at thy smile, or shadowed life know sunshine for a while. And so thy path shall be a track of light, like angels' footsteps passing through the night.

Be an angel!

CHAPTER 10

Heaven, Harps, Halos and Clouds

E ANGELS TO ONE ANOTHER ON EARTH. That's our challenge for today. But what about after we leave this earth? What then? Will we be given a harp, a halo and a cloud of our own?

> *I want to be an angel*
> *And with the angels stand*
> *A crown upon my forehead,*
> *A harp within my hand.*
>
> —URANIA BAILEY

Is that a fair request? Is it even a desirable one?

Dennis the Menace was debating the afterlife with Mr. Wilson. The issue was clouds. Do we each get our own? Can we visit one other?

Old Mr. Wilson began to panic at the possibility (however remote) of a celestial rendezvous with his earthly nemesis. Surely heaven wouldn't be like that?! But just in case, he gets the family Bible down from the shelf and begins frantically leafing through it.

Dennis: "What are you doing, Mr. Wilson?"
Wilson: "Looking for loopholes!"

Wilson's idea of heaven was not spending an eternity sharing a cloud with Dennis the Menace. Neither is it mine. Come to think of it, an eternity of harps, halos and a cloud (even my own) doesn't have a whole lot of appeal. If it does for you, you need to consider the fate of Mark Twain's ill-fated character, Captain Stormfield, who arrived at the pearly gates with such expectations only to have them quickly dashed when reality failed to match them.

Arriving confidently in paradise, Stormfield is shocked, disappointed and surprisingly vocal that things weren't in the order he had anticipated. Supposing himself to be an angel by this point, Stormfield boldly requests of St. Peter "everything that a body naturally requires up here"—a harp, wreath, halo, wings, palm branch and a fluffy white cloud upon which to perch in absolute bliss and glorious grandeur. Peter is truly puzzled and bothered, but finally gives in and provides Stormfield with a wardrobe becoming an angel and points him to a cloud. And confirming Mr. Wilson's nightmare, it is not his own. It is occupied by a million other "angels," who like Stormfield this day, have been arriving in heaven over the centuries clamoring for and receiving the same or similar endowments.

Undaunted, he settles in, gives his palm branch a wave for luck, tautens up his harp strings and sets to strumming. After sixteen or seventeen tedious hours of twanging the same tune over and over, the old gentlemen next to him finally has had enough.

"Don't you know any tune but the one you've been peggin' at all day?"
"Not another blessed one," says I.
"Don't you reckon you could learn another one?" says he.
"Never," says I; "I've tried to, but I couldn't manage it."

"It's a long time to hang to one—eternity, you know."

"Don't break my heart," says I; "I'm getting low-spirited enough already."

After a long silence, says he—"Are you glad to be here?"

Says I, "Old man, I'll be frank with you. This ain't just as near my idea of bliss as I thought it was going to be...."[1]

Hell (someone said, tongue in cheek) would be a whole lot better than a heaven of our own making. It's not completely true (the real hell is horrific, while harps and clouds are just plain boring—big difference!), but the point is well-taken. What any of us imagine heaven to be is bound to be a whole lot less than it will actually be. That's what makes the journey there so exciting—a journey Mark Twain himself unfortunately never embarked upon. He died the consummate skeptic, having aired his own attitudes through characters like Stormfield and others. When Miss Watson was telling Huck Finn that "all a body would have to do up there [the good place] was to go around all day long with a harp and sing, forever and ever," the young lad's nonchalence about the hereafter was equally indifferent: "So I didn't think much of it [either]."

An Extract from Captain Stormfield's Visit to Heaven tells us what Twain did think. Interestingly enough, it was his last published work (1909) before his death. On the good side, it is a humorous satirization of many of our conventional, albeit distorted, ideas of the life to come. But on the other hand, sadly, he does not provide, nor to my knowledge ever personally discover, a better end. It appears that Samuel Clemens (Twain's real name) held no hopes beyond the grave.[2]

And that's sad, because the Bible is clear that there is very real hope. Yes, he was right on the halo and harp debacle—we don't become angels in heaven. And yes, he gave us some accurate and necessary correctives and rightly humored us in the process. But he was tragically silent on an alternative. We needn't be.

So, what about heaven? What can we expect after death? How can we know for sure it involves us? We do not have the space to canvas the entire celestial picture in all its intricate and glorious splendor in these last pages, but we can certainly sketch some convincing basics to get you started on your journey there. To do that, let's look to the quintessential expert on angels. Who do you suppose knows more about angels than anyone else?

JESUS, ANGELS AND US

Jesus was a man whose earthly life was a mere thirty-something, and yet He witnessed more angelic action in His short life than all of us put together. You and I might well wonder about the activity of angels in our lives, but not Jesus. At every turn, angels were ready to respond to Him at His Father's bidding, be it one or an entire army. Consider this single telltale page out of His life from the New Testament. A suspense-filled night in a secluded ravine outside Jerusalem.

It has the makings for a very dark night. Only a thin ribbon of orange creases the horizon. Then the sun takes its last breath and inky blackness drops on the several figures scattered throughout the garden. The disciples and Jesus are there praying. Well, at least Jesus is. The rest have all fallen asleep. But He presses on.

Droplets of pinkish sweat bead like mercury drops from His forehead and mix with the tears streaming down His cheeks. He is weeping. He tries to pray, but the pain is so deep. The sound of His own voice is snuffed out by the muffled blanket of black pressing in on Him like a tight wet suit. It's a very dark night.

Never has He been so alone. Never has He felt so abandoned. What He has to do, no one else can do for Him. He is on his own. Judas will soon betray Him. His own people will arrest Him. Peter will deny Him. And to top it off, His inner circle, His last bastions of prayer support, are all asleep. And the cross is not far away. Even His own Father (God) is about to turn His back on Him. But not yet.

At some moment during the darkest hour, in a final, almost symbolic gesture of sympathy, the Father dispatches a single angel to the scene. It hovers protectively over the weary figure. Wipes His brow, His face, His hands. Embraces Him. Strengthens Him. Lifts Him up. Mysteriously, His energy begins to return.

Just then, the pounding of footsteps breaks the serenity and the angel flutters off. It's Judas the betrayer with his band of thugs waving lanterns, brandishing swords and clubs. As they begin to drag Jesus away, a scuffle ensues and the commotion awakens the disciples. Peter's sword is unsheathed and flashing before his feet hit the ground running. Everyone is ducking, jumping out of the way, but a servant of a high priest is a little slow and his ear gets in the way. Swoosh!

Jesus shouts and the mob freezes. "Peter! Put your sword away!"

Then turning to them all, with surprising calmness, adds confidently:

"Don't you realize that I am able right now to call to my Father, and twelve companies—more, if I want them—of fighting angels would be here, battle-ready?" (Matthew 26:53, *The Message*)

One night. One angel. And another 50 or 60,000 if He wanted them. Oh yes, Jesus knew all about angels. Why wouldn't He? Think about His life. Angels were all around the delivery room when He was born. They predicted His birth before it happened (Luke 1:30–38). They announced it to shepherds after it happened (2:8–15). But they didn't stop there.

Because of Herod the Great, His family escaped as Palestinian refugees to Egypt, thanks to an angel who forewarned His parents of the tetrarch's murderous intents to kill all babies under two years of age (Matthew 2:13). And then when Herod died, it was an angel who told them it was now safe to return home (2:19–20). From diapers to teething rings, angels were involved in Jesus' young life, predicting, announcing, forewarning and protecting. But they didn't stop there.

Later on as an adult, Jesus is attacked by Satan in the wilderness in a twisted and sinister attempt to destroy His power and disarm His ability to save the human race. After forty days of relentless conflict and no food, Jesus emerges victorious but emotionally and spiritually exhausted and physically famished. And angels came and attended to Him (4:11). On the heels of this supernatural renourishment, almost immediately, He returns to Galilee and begins His three years of public ministry. But they didn't stop there either.

Angels were present throughout His ministry and at various points during His life. And when He died and His body was placed securely in a tomb sealed with a huge stone, an angel descended on the scene. Scaring the Roman guards to unconciousness, he then rolled away the rock and perched upon it (28:2–4). When the women arrived to check on Jesus, the angel calmed their fears and announced Jesus' triumph over death, then quickly instructed them to go tell everyone else, which they did with great fear but greater joy! (28:5–8).

Angels were very busy surrounding the resurrection events of Jesus. But they don't stop there. Shortly after appearing alive to several people over a period of forty days, Jesus disappeared in a cloud into heaven. Everyone gasped as they stared into the empty sky. He was gone! "Suddenly two men appeared—in white robes! They said, 'You Galileans!—why do you just stand here looking up at an empty sky? This very Jesus who was taken up from among you to heaven will come as certainly—and mysteriously—as he left'" (Acts 1:10–11, *The Message*.) One day that empty sky will be full again—with Jesus and His angels who will accompany Him to gather believers together and usher them into the kingdom of heaven once and for all time (Matthew 24:31).

Jesus came to this planet—with angels. He lived on it—with angels. And the Bible tells He will come again to it—with angels.

But we missed something, didn't we? The cross. Did you ever notice? They stopped there. The angels were conspicuously absent when Jesus died. When Jesus needed the angels the most, He called the least.

You know what He could have done? He could have called 50, 60 or 100,000 to rescue Him. He could have called a trillion or two. But He didn't call a single one. He willingly forfeited all of His divine rights so that the Scriptures might be fulfilled—that He, the perfect sacrifice would necessarily spill His blood unassisted in order to pay the penalty for all sin for all mankind for all time. If even one angel would have swooped down—just one—and clipped a Roman guard with a single feather, the whole salvation plan would have been thwarted forever. But Jesus was silent. And so were the angels.

I can only imagine it took all the restraining power of heaven to hold them back. But hold they did. And Jesus died. Alone. For you. And for me. Because He did, you and I now have hope beyond the grave. A very real and glorious alternative to hell—even harps, halos and a cloud of our own for that matter. Because the angels were silent that one fateful night in history, human beings now have the invitation to be a party to everything that Jesus Himself ever shared or will share with the Father God. Everything. The apostle Peter was just as amazed as we should be:

> What a God we have! And how fortunate we are to have him, this Father of our Master Jesus! Because Jesus was raised from the dead, we've been given a brand-new life and have everything to live for, including a future in heaven—and the future starts now! God is keeping careful watch over us and the future. The Day is coming when you'll have it all—life healed and whole. (1 Peter 1:3–5, *The Message*)

Oh, yes. Jesus knew all about angels. And based on what He accomplished at the cross and verses like these (and there are many more—try Ephesians 1:3), we too can know, anticipate and experience the same blessings as He did (and does) including the ministry of angels in this life and the one to come. That's good news. In fact, it is the single reason the Bible was given to us—to guide people like you and me into not only a knowledge of intriguing information like this, but an actual experience and possession of it.

Here's how it works.

There is a certain chronology on which the Bible is very clear and dogmatic regarding all of this. Simply stated: Friend first, friends second. The number one most important thing a human being can do on this earth is to begin a relationship with God, to have a Friend in high places. A friendship with a million angels begins with a friendship with God.

Yes, the angels love you, I'm sure. But they are only extensions and vehicles of God's love. They can only demonstrate love to us as God releases them to serve us. Only God loves you endlessly and unconditionally. Only God demonstrated His love toward us in that while we were yet sinners, His Son died for us (Romans 5:8). Only God can enter a life, cleanse it and effect supernatural change there. The angels can't do that for you.

Should we respect them? Of course. Should we appreciate them? Definitely. Should we worship them? Absolutely not. Only God is to be worshiped for He alone has prepared and provided the reward we all seek. Yes, angels are present in heaven too, but they didn't make it. God did. And He provided the only way for you to get there—His Son, Jesus Christ. You can begin a friendship with Him today. It is freely offered. Will you freely receive it?

Putting my daughter to bed one night, she interrupted our Bible reading with: "Daddy, who is the real Jesus?" What a great question! I directed her to the picture in front of us. Jesus is surrounded by children. The caption read:

One day children were brought to Jesus in the hope that he would lay hands on them and pray over them. The disciples shooed them off. But Jesus intervened: "Let the children alone, don't prevent them from coming to me. God's kingdom is made up of people like these." (Matthew 19:14, *The Message*)

"Hmm. Where is Jesus now?" she then asked.

"Where do you think?"

"Up there?" she responded, pointing to the ceiling.

"Yes, but where else?"

"In our hearts!"

"Right, because you asked Him there, remember?"

She cocked her head sideways, then suddenly the conversation shifted to Winnie the Pooh, and the theology lesson was put on hold for another night.

But I got to thinking later that evening: there's one place where Jesus is not. Yes, God saturates infinity. He is omnipresent (everywhere all the time). And yet, mysteriously, there is one place where He is not. He is not in the heart where He has not been invited. He may extend His friendship, but you must accept. He's a gentleman and will not force Himself on anyone. Neither God nor the angels will interfere with your free will—the wherewithal to make choices for yourself. He offers. But it's your move.

How then, you may wonder, does one begin a friendship like this? From the very clear teachings of Scripture we can craft a simple composite prayer for beginning a friendship with God that will last an eternity. Perhaps it is one you might want to receive for yourself. So, receive it.

Jesus, I desire a friendship with You. I admit that because of the sin and shortcomings in my life I need You. I turn from those sins, all of them, and choose to follow You. Thank You for dying on the cross for me. Thank You for not calling the angels when You could have and I would have. Forgive me and cleanse me as only You can. I open myself to You and invite You into a place You've never been before but will never leave again from this day forward—my heart. Right this moment, in the best way I know how, I trust You to be my Friend forever. I accept You as my Savior and Forgiver. I allow You to be the Ruler of my life and gladly hand the reigns of it over to Your loving care. Help me, Lord Jesus Christ, to become the kind of person You created me to be. Amen (let it happen!).

When you look out into space, you look out into endlessness. And maybe you feel insignificant and small. But if you just prayed that prayer and meant it, the universe just shrunk. A big God has just come near to you. Meaning in life and a purpose for the living and dying of it has just come to you. Eternal life has just come to you. And, oh yes, the ministry of angels in this life and the expectation of cohabitation with them and your Creator and theirs in a future life has just come to you too. What that all looks like, well, we'll just have to wait and see. Some of it is telegraphed beautifully throughout Scripture. You can read the verses for yourself (try John 14:1–4 and Revelation 21:4 for starters). But before you do, let me assure you of one thing. It will be a whole lot better than halos and harps and sharing a cloud with Dennis the Menace. Count on it! Until then, remember, based on the promissory words of Jesus Himself:…[your] personal angels [**friends**] are constantly in touch with [your] Father [**Friend**] in heaven. (Matthew 18:10, *The Message*)

Angels: Friends in High Places. You literally need never leave home without them.

Introduction to Personal Stories

N 1996, *ALLIANCE LIFE* MAGAZINE invited readers to share personal experiences in which they believed God employed angels as His instruments in their lives. The response was overwhelming. Here, in their own words, are some of their stories.

The accounts are grouped under the various ministries (see "Job Description of an Angel, Parts I and II") that Scripture reveals angels have with human beings. Whether an angel or angels were involved in any or all of these incidents or not, we will never know for sure. Only God knows.

The secret things belong to the LORD our God, but the things revealed belong to us and to our children forever....

(Deuteronomy 29:29)

What we do know for sure, what does belong to us, is what is revealed to us in Scripture. And throughout its voluminous pages we have discovered that these are the kinds of things angels do. As such, there is no reason not to believe and expect that God in His providential love and wisdom will for these people and for you employ His angelic hosts to forewarn, strengthen, encourage, protect, defend, deliver, respond to prayers or provide comfort and assurance upon dying. And if and when any us of seems to have been touched by an angel in any of these ways, it is to God we direct our praise and thanksgiving, not the angels. If the truth were known, the angels are just as grateful to provide assistance as we are to receive it.

These stories, then, indeed this entire book, is a testament to God and God alone, for

> [He] has set his throne in heaven;
>   he rules over us all. He's the King!
> So bless God, you angels,
>   ready and able to fly at his bidding,
>   quick to hear and do what he says.
> Bless God, all you armies of angels,
>   alert to respond to whatever he wills.
> Bless God, all creatures, wherever you are
>   everything and everyone made by God.
> And you, oh my soul, bless God!
>   (David in Psalm 103:19–22, *The Message*)

Angels Announcing and Forewarning

Warning Signals

Miriam Charter

 HREE-AND-A-HALF YEARS after my first angelic "rescue" see "Lord, Help Me!"), I was back in the same bleak city in Northern Romania up near the Russian border. When I visited the pastor of the little church where I sometimes minister, I found him discouraged. That day a church in a town not faraway had been bulldozed by the authorities. The pastor of the church that was destroyed had called my friend from prison, pleading for help.

Grace, a fellow worker, and I spent that night in a dingy hotel, having arranged to be at the church the next day for a 1 p.m. meeting with a group of women. This meant a twenty-minute walk down the main street of town, a type of pedestrian mall. For many months this street had been torn up and new slabs of pavement were being put down.

As Grace and I cautiously picked our way along the uneven surface, the walkway narrowed so that only one person could pass at a time. We both stood aside to allow an elderly woman, holding tightly to the arm of a younger woman, to go by.

I was drawn to the kindness of the face of the younger woman. I could hardly take my eyes off her gentle features. As we went on our way, I became aware that she had left the older woman and was now following us.

In moments she was close behind us, and I heard her loudly clear her throat three times. I turned to see why she had done this, assuming she was seeking the attention of someone ahead of us. My eyes met hers, and she gestered wildly with one finger to turn sharply to the right. Because she was a total stranger and assuming the signal was for someone else, we continued to walk.

She moved even closer behind us, loudly clearing her throat three times. Again I looked around and our eyes met. With a desperate, pleading look, she gestured for me to turn right at the side street we were now opposite.

"Is she telling us to get off this main street," I whispered to Grace, "or is she luring us down this street to rob us? Perhaps the pastor sent her to warn us not to go to the church."

Again the young woman cleared her throat three times, and this time she placed two fingers above her eyes as if to say, "Someone is watching you." Once more she pointed down the street to our right and her eyes said, *"Please* obey me.

We turned off the mall and made our way down the side street. When I turned to see if the young woman was still following, she was nowhere to be seen.

Grace and I wandered around the area near the church for about an hour, debating whether it would endanger the pastor to go to his home. Finally we decided to risk it.

"Is everything all right?" I asked when we arrived. "Did you send someone to the mall to tell us not to come to the church an hour ago?" His sad face was full

of surprise. I described the young woman. Prognosis and sent my father to the
description.   inistered it to me with an eyedropper
   However, he went on to tell me that during ine the doctor's surprise to find me
involved with the secret police in the street y. He explained that, although the
militant force determined to bring about the ly hadn't fixed it and I would be
car and interrogated him for some time, eve
false charges. Had we not been interrupted e, my heart failure kept me in bed so
have arrived on the scene and further compain. Any excitement always proved
   My mind was filled with questions. Had e what the doctor termed "heart
messenger to redirect the path of His earthlot discussed prior to leaving so as not
   That night I felt strangely comforted and led.
near me as we made our way through the dble to attend only sporadically, my
had once again given His angels charge ove my frequent fainting spells, which

o recover for sometimes weeks on
hers who was very upset during one
ns to her all the time!" Years later, as I
ony that it was she who would soon
e never expected to live, was this

o attend only a few weeks. I was
rtness of breath and fatigue. One day,
astating heart attack. Again, I was
unconsciousness. The doctor informed
his long, he was sorry to tell them
ey were to make me as comfortable
e.

r's pronouncement, a man appeared at

Adapted by permission from *Alliance Life*, September 26,ild in the house and she told him there

was. The man offered a prayer and confidently told my mother that the child would be fine. She ran after him to thank him for his prayer and concern but, looking up and down the street, she found no trace of this stranger.

And then the angel came.

Lying in my bed one night, I was suddenly awakened by a bright light emanating from the right-hand corner of the room. It was like a sunbeam. As I watched, an angel appeared dressed in a white robe. There was a sword in his right hand and a heart in the other one. The heart was red like blood.

The angel quietly approached my bed. He made a painless cutting motion on my left side under my arm, took out the old heart and put in the new one. He touched the place where the "cut" was and it healed immediately. I was awake and unafraid the entire time. Then, as quickly as he came, he disappeared into the light beam.

I started laughing and crying. Mother came running into the room thinking that surely I was dying. I told her that God had just sent an angel to give me a new heart. She tried to calm me down, fearing I would stress my heart too much. I relaxed and fell asleep—a peaceful, restful sleep.

From that time on I kept getting better and better. I told everyone that God had given me a new heart and many people looked at me like I was making it up. An older gentleman from our church came to visit. When I told him about my experience, he looked at me and told me never to doubt the healing power of God and to keep praising and thanking Him for this miracle.

Years later, my adult daughter told me that doctors routinely ask patients if they have had any history of heart disease.

"If you are ever asked that question, Mother," she said, "perhaps you should refrain from telling the angel story or you may be misdiagnosed with senile dementia!"

Sure enough. Not many days later, a doctor asked me if I had any history of heart disease.

"I certainly do," I said, ignoring my daughter's advice. I then proceeded to tell him my story. After extensive cardiac testing, he said, "If God fixed it, He fixed it good. You have absolutely no sign of having any heart problems!" To God be the glory!

Myrtle A. Hamm Robinson is a widowed mother of two, grandmother of five, and great-grandmother of eight. God's miracle allowed her to live a full and productive life, which included graduating from Nyack Missionary Training Institute, attending Arkansas Technical College, completing cosmotology school, owning and operating her own business, earning a Bachelor of Science degree in elementary education at the age of forty-nine, and finishing her master's degree at the age of fifty-two.

Yohan and the Angel

Daniel G. Larson and Gordon F. Larson

YOHAN MURIP WAS A DANI EVANGELIST, teacher, Bible translator, church administrator—and much more. Everything he undertook seemed to prosper and was done in a timely manner with enthusiasm and for the glory of God. He was God's instrument—God's arrow, if you will—never swerving to the right or left, always on target and shot regularly by our Lord to fell the forces of evil in the deep valleys of Irian Jaya (formerly called Dutch New Guinea).

And then he was gone.

Yohan died of malaria on June 21, 1983. He was about thirty-five years of age and only three-and-a-half years into an extensive and effective ministry. Traveling from valley to valley, he preached to thousands and witnessed the miraculous: healings, conversions of war leaders long resistant to the message of Jesus Christ—and encounters with angelic beings.

Yohan had a humble beginning in a remote region of the central highlands of Irian Jaya. His people, the Western Dani, at that time had yet to be discovered by the outside world. They were still using stone axes, participating in tribal warfare and periodically appeasing ancestral and nature spirits to maintain land fertility, insure good health and initiate their young men into the sacred cult of the Dani tribe.

However, in December of 1958, the Western Dani made a dramatic move. Impacted by the arrival of Christian missionaries, and following the lead of their Damal neighbors, those residing in the Ilaga Valley began to burn their sacred objects as evidence of their break with animism and commitment to Christ. The "burning movement" spread to encompass most of the 130,000 Danis residing in scores of isolated valleys.

Yohan was just a lad of about twelve when we first met him. In an effort to teach the thousands who were coming to faith in Jesus Christ we established a "witness school." The first class consisted of twenty couples who came to study during the week, then returned to their respective home areas on weekends to teach what they had learned. On Sundays they returned en masse for an all-day teachathon involving two to three thousand people. Yohan learned to read, began attending the witness school and eventually, after completing Bible school and serving as a teacher and pastor, studied for three years at the Jaffray School of Theology.

In 1983 while preaching in the Beoga valley, Yohan had an encounter, a supernatural manifestation, which Wondagaloogwe, his cousin and songleader, described as follows:

> One afternoon, Yohan suggested we climb up the mountainside to an
> isolated spot near the forest to pray. While praying some distance from
> each other, I suddenly heard a rushing sound like a whirlwind.

At first I thought it might be an airplane, but concluded that was impossible because of the heavy cloud cover and because airplanes do not fly low in such rugged terrain in the late afternoon.

I looked up and over toward Yohan. Near him there was what looked like a rainbow with a flame twisting upward in a whirlwind, something similar to what Elisha must have seen when Elijah was taken up into heaven.

Although filled with fear, I got up and went over to Yohan.

"Did you see it also?" he asked. "It's an angel. He comes periodically to minister to me."

That night at the meeting, hundreds connected significantly with God. Some were healed. Others confessed their sins and were restored to fellowship with God.

We have pondered long over what caused Yohan to accomplish so much in such a short time and with such powerful manifest approval from the Lord.

The answer, we believe, lies in his steadfastness and dedication to a life of faith and prayer. Even as a teenager attending the witness school, he built himself a grass-roofed hut near the forest to get away from the distractions of the communal men's house so he could pray and meditate alone. While at Bible school, he built similar prayer huts, and when he attended graduate school in the crowded city of Ujung Pandang, we are told he would rise early to climb onto a branch of a nearby banyan tree to seek the Lord in seclusion.

Even Yohan's homegoing was miraculous. He repeatedly said he would meet the Lord in person in 1983. Audiences always interpreted this as a conviction that the Lord would return in 1983. Instead, for reasons unknown to us, the Lord saw fit to take Yohan to Himself.

His body was brought for burial to a site central to the valley near where the Dani witness school stood and where he first learned about his Lord. His relatives buried him on a nearby hillside in standing position, with Bible in hand, ready to meet the Lord, whom he loved, at His coming.

The House Call
Cecil M. Smith

MY WIFE EUNICE AND I were spending a few days with our son Ben at a conference on the coast of Ecuador. One day at the afternoon coffee break, we all joined our kids for a few leisurely minutes.

Ben was still small enough for me to carry on my back. So, on our way to the dining hall for snacks, I picked him up and put him on my shoulders. But when I went to stand up, I couldn't straighten my back. I had slipped a disc.

After coffee, as I took my place at the secretary's table, the chairman noticed I was in pain and asked for some of our colleagues to pray for me. I received a measure of relief at that moment but knew that things were still not right with my back.

After the evening meeting we all found our places in the bamboo dormitories for another night of rest. Again I prayed.

During the night I was awakened by hands on my back doing a kind of chiropractic adjustment. At first I thought it was my wife. She had gone through a number of crises with my chronic back problems and was always comforting and helpful.

But I could see that she was in front of me facing the other way and in a deep sleep. Son Benjamin was in his own bed.

I turned to see who had invaded our room in the middle of the night. No one was there, but I sensed a wonderful feeling of peace from the "presence" as the invisible hands finished the adjustment. Almost simultaneouly I heard my bones go back into place and realized that this had to be the work of an angel—an angel with chiropractic skills. There was no other explanation.

Adrift on a Cloud
Anne M. Dick

IT WAS MAY 1990. Curled up in a fetal position, I was in so much pain that I longed for death. Although I had been severely afflicted for twenty-two years with rheumatoid arthritis, I felt I was now dealing with something very wrong internally.

My husband, in total desperation, finally took me to the emergency area of our local hospital. After several days of testing, probing and consulting several specialists, I was diagnosed with empyema—one lung was totally infected. The doctors informed me that they would have to do a thoracentisis, which involved removing one of my ribs. He also cautioned me that there was a high risk due to the severity and length of the infection and the arthritis medications I was taking.

The sweet, serene peace God gave me was indescribable. My husband and I prayed together with our family and we said our special farewell. I believed that soon I would be with Jesus—no more pain, no tears, no sorrow—only praise with a new, whole body.

What a disappointment when I awoke and found myself in a hospital bed surrounded by tubes, needles and machines bubbling antibiotics through my lung. I was very weak and in unspeakable pain.

Instantly I was enveloped in what appeared to be a white filmy shroud. At each corner was an angel. Together they gently lifted me off the bed and held me suspended in air.

"We'll carry you. We'll carry you. Fear not," they whispered.

Suddenly I was pain free and seemed to be adrift on free-floating clouds. It was wonderful, amazing, comforting. This continued for four days and nights, then they were gone. But during that time I had received enough strength to put my hands in the hands of my Lord and to endure three weeks of constant antibiotic flushing of my lungs.

Since then I have had several surgeries. Although I longed once again for some reassurance of the visible angels, my request was not granted. Instead, I knew joy and peace in my heart and understood that Jesus Himself was interceding for me when I could only groan.

I will always praise God for His wonderful, mysterious ways and for that special visible glimpse of His heavenly messengers.

Angel Watching over Her
Sandy Brown

THIRTY YEARS AGO we had never heard of anyone seeing an angel. My husband and I knew very little about the supernatural. During that time, we grieved for a child we had lost through an undiagnosed internal birth defect. It was an empty, painful period in our lives.

In my teenage years the idea of adopting a child became a burning desire in my heart. Perhaps now my dream could become a reality. Being young and naive, we even dared to tell God that He would have to produce the child of our dreams by August 1 or we would forget the whole idea.

The last day of July was a Saturday. We knew that the adoption agency was closed on Saturdays and Friday had already passed with no hope of a baby.

Deeply disappointed, we assumed that another dream had come to an end. Then the phone rang! It was our caseworker. She said she did not normally work on Saturdays, but something had come up and she wondered if we would mind coming to her office to complete our remaining interviews.

Ten days later, we called a pediatrician to arrange an appointment for the child we were to receive the following day. Our doctor cautiously advised us, "Are you sure you really want to adopt a child this soon? You are not over mourning the loss of your little boy. Please take time to think it over carefully." We didn't have to think very long.

We took home a beautiful baby girl. Once again, I asked God to please confirm this was the child He had chosen for us. Having cuddled, loved and adored her all day, we finally tucked her into her little bed, but a heaviness once again struck my heart. *Was this child really the one God had for us?*

Later that night, as I was walking down the hall by her room, my eye caught something unusual. There was a body of light next to her crib. I stopped briefly, then walked downstairs to the kitchen. When finally I went back, the angelic being was still there, now bent over the child.

I passed by and went into the master bedroom. My husband was sitting on the edge of the bed with tears in his eyes.

"You saw the angel, too, didn't you?" he asked.

That event happened thirty years ago. And that beautiful child has been a great blessing to us. When times were hard and fear reached out to grip my heart as she faced difficult days, my confidence was renewed as God brought to my memory the image of the angel bending over my little girl.

Angel at the Bus
Derek L. Hastings

JANUARY 5, 1980, DAWNED cold and cloudy, snow gently falling on the empty street. Only a few days earlier I had publicly acknowledged Jesus Christ as my Lord and Savior. And today I was to catch a city bus that would take me to the Port Authority in New York City and on to coast guard training in Yorktown. Nancy and I moved slowly, trying not to think of the four months we would be apart.

Finally, with my duffel bag, a carry-on and my new Bible in the car, we headed for the bus station. About five minutes before the bus was scheduled to arrive, I realized I had left my uniform hat back at the house. Nancy jumped in the car and drove back to get it, leaving me to wait for the bus. By the time she returned, I had missed the bus that would have allowed me to make connections in New York.

I finally boarded the next "86" and arrived at the Port Authority precisely at 10:30. I jumped off in a panic, my mind swimming with images of showing up late for Officer Candidate School.

Once inside, I found the ticket area, got in line and bought my ticket. My bus, they said, was leaving from Gate 36. I ran the full length of the building before I saw a sign that indicated that Gate 36 was downstairs and all the way back at the other end.

I glanced down at my watch. It was 10:45 and there were no people waiting in line! I crashed into the metal door with all the weight of my body and luggage. There sat the bus, engine idling.

"Is this the bus to Baltimore?" I asked breathlessly as the driver opened the door.

"Yes, it is," he replied.

The man climbed down from his seat and proceeded to the cargo compartment to stow my bag. He was a big man, over six feet tall with broad shoulders, a big smile and white hair. As I turned to climb into the bus, he asked, "What's that book you have there?"

"It's my new Bible," I replied. "I just bought it last weekend."

The driver smiled.

"Read Psalm 91:11 and you will see why I waited for you."

"What?" I exclaimed, exhausted from the excitement.

"Read Psalm 91:11 and you will see why I waited for you."

I climbed on board, found a seat on the left side about halfway back near the window and opened my Bible. "For he will command his angels concerning you to guard you in all your ways."

I looked up. The driver was watching me in the large rearview mirror.

"Beautiful, isn't it?" he said as our eyes met.

Sometime later, in Baltimore, I watched as the bus pulled out of the station and stopped at a traffic signal a short distance down the road. The driver turned, locked eyes with me and, with another big smile, waved. Amazed, I waved back.

When I finally reached the motel, I called Nancy and told her about the incident on the bus.

"Maybe the man was your guardian angel," she suggested.

At first such a thing was difficult to believe, but when I thought about it, I realized that I had not pre-purchased my tickets and no one knew I was coming. Although I arrived almost fifteen minutes past the departure time, the driver said he had specifically waited just for me! And, what's more, he had waited because God had commanded His angel to guard me along my way.

Throughout the years I have held on to this memory as a very personal and special gift from my Heavenly Father. I believe the Lord sent His angel to establish in my heart whose child I had become.

Peace Angel

Peggy Allen Gunther

SAIGON, 1969. ANOTHER EARLY MORNING random rocket attack literally shook us awake! The rapidity and proximity startled us. With our two young daughters Kathy and Missy, we scrambled to a safer area in the middle of the apartment.

Only a few days before, the communists had attempted to blow up a radio station just a block from us. As a result of the explosion, the curtains on our windows stood straight out horizontally and a spent bullet ricocheted off our dining room wall, landing on the floor by the front door. Not one of us, including some guests, was touched.

Now, huddling together yet again on that early morning in 1969, we squeezed into the center hall. *Another potentially frightening experience for two-year-old Kathy,* I thought sadly. *What are we doing here, anyway?* It was time for a gentle reminder from God that His angels would not allow anything to touch our lives apart from His will. It would be many years before I found out what really happened that day.

From her viewpoint in the hall, Kathy had one advantage over the rest of us—she could see into the living room. There, sitting in our rocking chair, was a man reading a newspaper, his form outlined by colored lights like those on a Christmas tree.

Many years would pass before Kathy told us the story of the man in the rocking chair.

"When I saw that man," she told us, "I wasn't afraid anymore."

A young woman now, Kathy's account of her *peace angel* is just as vivid as when she was that little girl. In the crisis of the moment, in the din of explosions, God opened the eyes of one of His children. No one else saw her angel, but peace came to the heart of a frightened little girl.

The "Hallelujah Chorus"
with Extra Notes
Deborah L. Byrne

BECAUSE IT WAS WAY PAST BEDTIME, I was surprised when nine-year-old Nathan called me into his room.

"What is keeping you awake?" I asked him, thinking that pre-Christmas excitement was preventing sleep.

"I am feeling rebellious," he answered, using a word almost bigger than his small stature. "I don't know whether to believe that Jesus is real or if my prayers even matter."

I paused, somewhat taken aback by the rather adult response.

How could he doubt? Nathan had often heard the story about his precarious start in the world. Born three months premature, he had weighed only two pounds. Limp and blue and unable to breathe on his own, a faint, thready heartbeat was the only sign of life.

Although the antibiotics that coursed through his veins were efficient germ killers, they were known to be toxic to the delicate parts of the inner ear, often leaving premature infants with hearing impairment.

But a faithful God reached down and not only preserved Nathan's life, but brought him through innumerable crises. Our church, our family and countless others prayed earnestly and we were rewarded with not only a normal, but an extraordinary boy.

At the age of five, Nathan started piano lesssons. His hearing was particularly acute. He also had perfect pitch and could identify any note he heard. At the age of six he called out of the bedroom, "That music on the TV is in the key of D minor." It was!

Piano lessons continued and by the time Nathan was nine, he could play Handel's "Hallelujah Chorus." Barely able to reach the pedals or stretch his hand to an octave, he played the piece with wings on his fingers and an easy grin on his face.

That night in his bedroom, after a brief out-loud prayer asking for God's truth and peace to comfort Nathan and to help him go to sleep, I put my hands on him and asked that God's spiritual forces would conquer the fears and doubts the enemy was whispering to him. I included a request that God's angels would surround Nathan, assuring him of his safety.

When I finished, Nathan was crying.

"Mommy, I feel so much better," he said as he reached out to hug me. I left the room, confident that sleep would come soon in the peaceful dark of the winter night.

"Mommy, do you ever hear voices?" Nathan asked the next morning.

I forced a patronizing smile.

"What kind of voices, Nathan?" I said, pausing to kneel beside him on the floor.

"Well," he said, looking me squarely in the eye, "last night after you prayed and left my room I heard voices."

"Yes?" I waited.

"My room was filled with angels. They were dressed in white robes like we wore in the Christmas play, but their wings were shiny and beautiful. They were singing the 'Hallelujah Chorus.' But Mommy, it was different than any choir sings—they sang with extra notes!"

Because Nathan has perfect pitch and knows the musical score to that magnificent piece, he had discerned their angelic harmonization. To our precious son—and to us—this was another sign that God hears and answers prayer.

Angels Protecting and Defending

Angels versus the Khmer Rouge
Bernard Dunning

AKEO I REFUGEE CAMP was located in eastern Thailand fifty kilometers from the Thai/Cambodian border. Volunteers under the United Nations and the International Red Cross maintained the camp from 8 A.M. to 6 P.M. But from 6 P.M. until 8 A.M. the Cambodian Khmer Rouge (communists) were in control.

By the time my wife Edythe and I arrived at the camp in January 1980, the refugee count had mounted to over 33,000 within three months. Their condition had certainly improved healthwise, but mentally it was deteriorating. Now that they were feeling physically stronger, there was a great desire to be free. The overseers of the camp, however, had other ideas.

The Khmer Rouge announced that they were planning to relocate the refugees back to their homeland, Cambodia. Those who volunteered to go back on the first exodus would be guaranteed a bed to sleep on. Those who volunteered for the second stage would have the ground to sleep on. Nothing at all could be guaranteed for the third group of volunteers. Buses and trucks for the journey back to the Cambodian border would be provided by the Khmer Rouge.

Their plan to make the move in three stages was actually only a ploy to frighten the people into signing up to fight for the Khmer Rouge. But the effect was just the opposite: refugees began searching for other ways to get out from under their control.

During the first month we were in the camp, I conducted five services a day in the longhouses. Sometimes a "secret meeting" was held for the people to tell me what was taking place in the camp. The conclusion was always the same: nobody wanted to go back to Cambodia to fight for the Khmer Rouge.

It was announced that on February 2 buses and trucks were coming to transport the first group of volunteers and that ten days later the second trip would take place. It was also announced that all those who were Buddhists and Christians, those who were teaching at the camp school and all interpreters would be killed.

February 2 came and went. Nothing happened.

About the middle of February we noticed that the Khmer Rouge followers were wearing their black uniforms again. They were also carrying cloth bags filled with rice, no doubt hoarded from the camp supplies. Others showed their sympathies by wearing colored clothing.

Christians were receiving hand-written notes such as, "We'll be back for you. Your blood must cover the soil of Cambodia." Night meetings (controlled by the Khmer Rouge) were becoming regular events at the camp. Christians and rebellious nonbelievers were often punished or embarrassed as examples to others to obey the Khmer Rouge. The Christians counted this a great privilege and opportunity to suffer for the cause of Christ.

They decided that once we knew when an exodus would take place, all those in the back of the camp would move to the front to sleep with other believers.

When the day of the proposed exodus arrived, the Christian leaders spent the afternoon organizing the move. I must admit I was anxious to get back to the camp the next morning to see what had happened.

As we approached the camp, we knew right away that something was wrong. No one was at the gate to meet us. And inside the gates, people walked around the camp as though they did not see us. I went to a classroom as usual. The Christian leaders were already gathered there. I greeted them. The response lacked their regular enthusiasm.

"What happened last night?" I asked.

Silence. They pointed to one of the men to act as their spokesman. By now my heart was racing.

He told me that after we had left at 6 P.M. soliders appeared throughout the camp. By 8 P.M. they were carrying guns. Although dressed like American soldiers, some of them spoke perfect Cambodian.

They said words like, "Do not be afraid; we are here to protect you," and other such phrases. The soldiers, they said, had left just before 8 A.M.

"Where were the Khmer Rouge soldiers while all this was happening?" I asked. Appaently they had remained in their longhouses all night.

After discussing this unusual turn of events, we prayed and divided up into groups to walk through the camp to see if any Christians were missing. I also sent word for the UN representative to come and see me. When he arrived, I told him what I had heard.

He said he knew nothing about soldiers being in the camp. Neither did he know that the Khmer Rouge had been planning to leave the camp for Cambodia. He promised to phone Bangkok to find out who had authorized the soldiers to be there.

The next morning when we arrived at the camp, the Christians told us that the soldiers had appeared again. Once more I asked to meet with the UN representative. He was shocked to learn that the soldiers had returned.

"John, you know your Bible and you remember the story of Elisha, how God sent heavenly hosts to protect him. Well, don't you believe that God would do it again to protect the believers here in the camp?" I asked.

"But you know no one will believe it," he responded.

"I believe it!" I said.

The next night the soldiers returned to the camp and once again the Khmer Rouge soldiers stayed in their longhouses.

"I would like to see one of the soldiers," I told a believer.

"Well, you have to be here after 6 P.M."

About 5 o'clock that afternoon, the evangelistic team was returning to the front of the camp, preparing to leave.

"Look, said one of the men, "there are two of those soldiers."

I turned in the direction the man was pointing. About 100 feet away were two soldiers. I dropped everything and started running. The soldiers appeared to be talking with four or five men and boys. I greeted one of them and touched his elbow. He turned toward me. At the same time, the other soldier started to walk away.

"Sir," a man said, "they don't speak Cambodian."

"What language do they speak?" I asked. In that moment both soldiers turned and walked away. We started after them as they headed between two rows of longhouses. But when we got there, the soldiers were gone. Although there were no entrances or exits in any of the houses on either side of the row, they simply were nowhere to be seen.

We asked the people in the area if they had seen any soldiers.

The answer was negative.

On Sunday, March 16, my wife and I were in Bangkok on our way home to the States. The UN representative, who had been working in Bangkok since the failure of the great exodus, had at my urging checked on three things: (1) were there really plans for a mass exodus from the camp? (2) were the Thai and

Khmer Rouge working together to provide buses and trucks? and (3) had American soldiers been sent to stop the exodus?

He reported that it was true that an exodus had been planned for that night. The buses and trucks, he said, were to have been there at 8 P.M., but officals could not find out why they had not left for the camp.

"And what about the soldiers?" I asked.

"There is no evidence of soldiers being sent to the camp."

"But soldiers were there. We have the proof," I replied.

He smiled and said, "The report says that there is no evidence of soldiers being sent to the camp."

If there were no soldiers, why was the exodus called off?

Only God knows the answer to that question.

The angel of the LORD *encamps around those who fear him, and he delivers them.* (Psalm 34:7)

Angels at Ramangord
Frances Emery

SLEEP WAS SLOW IN COMING that December night as I mentally reviewed the Christmas story I would be telling the children in church the next morning. Only the cry of a distant jackal broke the stillness of the jungle night.

The villagers had long since gone to bed. No babies were crying. Even the pie-dogs had ceased their yapping. Just outside the Indian village of Ramangord, our missionary camp was safely asleep in their homemade trailer and tents.

But what a different scene greeted us in the early hours the following morning.

"Did you see them? Are you safe? Who was it? What happened?" Our sleepy helper was making his way to the nearby stream for water when voices and the sound of running feet caught his attention. The villagers wanted to know if he too had seen the "men?"

It was a time of turmoil in the state of Hyderabad, India. A struggle for power between Hindus and Muslims was complicated by the addition of still another group, the radical Razakars. They were not a religious movement, only power-seeking troublemakers determined to take advantage of the situation.

Just one week earlier they had overturned a bus in a nearby village, burning it and many of the passengers in it. They were feared by all in the region. And here we sat, in our little camp, my husband and I, our two sons home from boarding school for Christmas vacation, and our young daughter. Also in the group was the Indian pastor, his wife and children, plus the camp cook and his wife and son.

What had we not seen? Whom had we not heard? Had the Razakars come and harmed the village? Finally we were able to make out some of the words being hurled at us: Razakar, fire, gone.

As the villagers began to catch their breath and settle down enough to tell us what had happened, the facts began to emerge. Men had come in the night, a large group of them. They were headed for our camp. Then, suddenly, they all stopped, turned and ran away as fast as they could go, dropping their lanterns, sticks, kerosene tins—everything they were carrying—the only testatment to a near disaster.

The villagers were awakened by the commotion but wisely let them go. But why the sudden retreat?

To the utter amazement of all, the villagers reported that they had seen what the Razakars must also have seen. Around the little camp in the mango grove was a circle of "men," facing outward, each one holding a lantern that glowed red. Never before had anyone seen a red lantern. Before the villagers could reach the camp, the "men" disappeared.

Pastor Jacobu's Christmas message that day included, as expected, the message of the angels: "A Savior is born." But that Christmas, the story took on new meaning. The entire village of Ramangord had themselves seen angels. Our family was privileged to see only the items they had left behind.

And we were grateful that God had given His angels charge over us, to keep us safe in an Indian mango grove.

Angels in the Gulch
Lyle Eggleston

JUAN CONONAO LIVED WITH HIS FAMILY in a small town in southern Chile. A full-blooded Mapuche Indian, Juan was the pastor of a small church. One of his weekly Bible classes was held in a farmhouse about a mile outside town. Since Juan had neither a bicycle nor a saddle horse, his habit was to walk across the field, down a gulch and back up through a pasture to the parishioners' home.

In the same town, there was a man who hated Pastor Juan, not because of anything Juan had done, but simply because he was an ardent believer in Jesus Christ.

The would-be assassin later told this story.

"Determined to kill pastor Juan, I decided to hide in the brush at the bottom of the draw Juan always crossed on his way to and from the farmhouse.

On this particular night, I was there, waiting for Juan to return from the meeting. It was easy to tell when he was coming, for Juan had the custom of singing hymns as he walked.

"When he arrived at the edge of the gulch, I cocked by pistol and waited. Then a strange thing happened. As Juan descended into the gulch, other voices joined in his hymn. The singing became louder and louder as they came closer.

"Not wanting to confront that many people, I relaxed my grip on the pistol. The singers passed by. Then, in an instant, as the group climbed out of the gulch, all of the voices stopped except that of Pastor Juan."

I believe there is no other way to explain this incident except to say that a choir of angels joined Juan in the gulch that night. And, by doing so, they saved his life.

Angels—A Part of Life

Oliver J. Abrams

THROUGHOUT A LIFETIME OF MINISTRY, first as a pastor in northern California, and then for thirty-seven years as a missionary in the Philippines, I have at various times been the recipient of God's love and protection through His ministering angels. Let me share a few instances with you.

It was the fall of 1967. As pastor of the Hayfork Bible Church, I volunteered to clean the church chimney in preparation for winter. The building was a typical wooden structure with a steep "snow country" galvanized roof. At the back was a flat-roofed lobby area. The chimney was located about ten feet up the roof near the lobby end of the building.

On the ground to the side of the lobby was a pile of unremoved refuse accumulated from a fall cleanup, but never disposed of. Next to it was a four-foot square patch of clean, soft grass directly below where the church roof connected with the lobby roof.

With a gunnysack weighted by a chain, about twenty-five feet of rope, and a ladder, I proceeded to climb onto the lobby roof. The problem now was how I would get up onto the church roof. Never having been a country-roof chimney sweep before, I picked up the gunnysack and rope and climbed up to the chimney. It was more of a struggle than I anticipated but I made it.

Once the "sweeping the chimney" task was completed, I began to think about how I would get down. Up to that point, I had not given it much thought.

The distance from the chimney to the lobby roof going down looked a lot more challenging than it had coming up. *If I made it safely up, surely I can make it safely down!* I thought to myself. It never occurred to me to attach the rope to the chimney and use it as a safety rope. Instead I threw the gunnysack and rope down onto the lobby roof.

Letting go of the chimney, I lunged my body toward the lobby roof. However, once released to the pull of gravity, instead of heading for the flat roof, I found myself aimed straight for the edge of the steep roof. At the bottom lay that hazardous pile of unremoved garbage.

I was standing erect by the time I reached the edge of the roof. At that point, I felt my fall intercepted by two unseen but nevertheless real "men" who took the thrust of my projecting body full on their chests. I slid off the bodies and landed still standing upright and unhurt on that God-provided, soft and grassy spot.

Sitting down to recover, I thanked and praised God for the guardian angels whom He had that day charged with the responsibility of keeping me "in all my ways."

Another incident took place during a trip home. My mother's older sister was very special to all our family. Going to Tanta's house for vacations and other family affairs was always a greatly anticipated treat. Next to seeing my own parents after five years, the number one priority on arriving in America was to pay a visit to Tanta.

I had not driven a car since our last furlough (visit to our homeland) and none of our previous vehicles had had an automatic transmission. Our furlough car would be a new experience.

After two weeks with my parents on Long Island, my wife, our five children and I headed to the Pennsylvania countryside to see Tanta.

Leading off an access road, the steep incline up to Tanta's house ended in a circle that followed a "stay right" traffic pattern. It was tradition that, before doing anything else, visitors would go to the house to greet Tanta who was usually waiting on her small porch. I was anxious for her to see how our children had grown, so I hurriedly parked the car at the top of the driveway.

After our greetings, I turned to go and begin the unpacking. To my horror, I saw the car begin to move forward. I knew immediately what was wrong. I had left the gearshift in neutral instead of putting it in park.

I ran toward the car, which, by the time I reached it, had begun a full roll down the hill. Opening the driver's door, I grabbed the steering wheel and tried to pull myself onto the seat. I missed. The middle post hit me and knocked me down. Having in the process pulled the steering wheel to the left, I watched as the car began to roll, not down the driveway, but toward a rock fence where, it seemed, it would inevitably crash.

Holding the steering wheel with my right hand as my body dragged along, I could feel the car gaining momentum. Strange as it may seem, the saying "the Lord helps those who helps themselves" came to mind. Realizing that the rock fence was fast approaching, I said to myself, "I had better try to do something about this."

As I tried to pull myself upright, "something" picked me up bodily and placed me, sitting, in the dirver's seat!

"Hey, I'm in the driver's seat!" I exclaimed. the element of "this is unbelievable" passed in an instant. Now, in full control of the runaway car, I managed to stop it safely before it hit the rock wall.

There is no doubt in my mind that an angel of the Lord placed me in the driver's seat that day.

Back in the Philippines once again, we were setting up housekeeping for our third term. The local furniture stores were well stocked. Although not too spacious, many of them had a mezzanine level that extended about half the length of the ground floor. It was usually not walled in and, as it turned out, the particular store I chose did not have even a guardrail to protect people from the twelve-foot drop.

When I didn't find anything I wanted on the main floor, the salesman suggsted we move to the upper floor. There was nothing there I wanted either, so, deciding to visit another store, I stepped back to turn to go down the stairs.

As I did, I felt a sharp finger-thrust in my left kidney area. Thinking that I had bumped into the salesman, I turned to apologize. But he was about six feet to my left. I, however, was standing on the very edge of the mezzanine floor. Another step backward would have resulted in my falling to the main floor below.

I sensed immediately that the hand thrust had come from a guardian angel to warn me of the potential danger. Once again, God had sent a ministering spirit to watch over me.

As a district missionary in the Philippines, I was frequently called upon to visit our churches for special occasions and Bible conference ministries.

On this particular Sunday, I was to preach both at a rural church and a town church, about eight miles from each other. About two miles from my starting point there was a river and a transportation terminal providing an assortment of vehicles to the interior. The trip from the river to the town was six miles.

A jeep was waiting when I arrived and the trip to the interior went without incident. The worship service was wonderful and, after the noon meal featuring Filipino delicacies at their best, I headed back to the town.

A large crowd was at the interior terminal, twice as many as any vehicle should carry. But because there is "always room for one more" on commercial vehicles in the Philippines, everyone piled on. Thinking to set a good example, I decided to let them go ahead. I would wait for the next jeep. A number of others stayed also and we visited happily for about a half hour. It was approaching 2:30 and I began to wonder if I would make it back to town for the 7 o'clock service.

Finally I asked one of the men who was with me what time the next jeep was due to arrive. His answer? There would not be another jeep! I asked him what they were going to do about getting to town.

"We are not going to town," he responded. "We are just waiting here with you!"

How, then, was I to get to town? I was in excellent physical shape and could walk a consistent fifteen-minute mile. Since I was traveling light I knew I could walk those six miles to the river in about three hours. That would land me back at the church about 6 o'clock. Bidding my simpathetic friends good-bye, I started off on the road to the river.

Suddenly, as I walked along, I began to realize that I was not alone. I sensed the presence of angels with me. What's more, I sensed that I was gliding along rather than walking. The landscape arund me seemed to be an animation, moving past me as if I were standing still. By this time I knew I was being assisted by angelic companions. Time and distance became insignificant as I thrilled in the presence of these heavenly beings God had sent.

Soon I was at the river. Just as I reached the near edge, the jeep that had left a half hour before me from six miles in the interior was pulling up out of the river on the far side!

It was then that my traveling companions left me to normal conditions. Once across the river, I hitched a ride along with many others in an empty dump truck, and was back in town in ample time to eat supper and get to the evening service.

For me, angels seem to be a part of life.

The Unseen Protector

Dorothy M. Hostetter

SEVERAL YEARS AGO ON OUR WAY to Maine, my friend Alda Greeley and I stayed overnight with a friend in the Burlington, Vermont area. The trip had been uneventful and, after visiting and catching up on the news, Alda and I retired for the night.

Miss Greeley's home had been in Maine until she moved to New York City. "Greeley," as she was affectionately known, and I were staying in the same room.

Shortly after midnight, I heard her get up and asked where she was going.

"I'm heading for the bathroom," she responded.

She wasn't gone long when I heard a noise. I bounded out of bed and began searching down the hall. There was no sign of her in any of the rooms where the doors were open, including the bathroom. I walked as far as the kitchen and living room. No Greeley.

That left only two possibilities. One door led to the room of our hostess and the other to the basement. Both were closed.

About that time, our hostess appeared. That left only the basement door unchecked. We opened the door. Sure enough! There was Greeley in a heap at the bottom of the open-sided stairway.

"Please help me get up," she begged.

Many thoughts raced through my mind. Did she have any broken bones?

How would I get her up the steps? Would she have to be hospitalized? If so, where was the nearest hospital?

I scurried to the bottom of the steps. When she assured me that she was all right, I asked her if she could walk up the steps.

Confidently she replied, "Yes, If you help me get up."

I quickly checked her over. Nothing seemed to be broken, so up the steps she walked with me directly behind her. When we reached the top and found a place for her to sit, she asked me to pray. I was still somewhat breathless, so she prayed, thanking the Lord for His care.

We checked her again. Finding no apparent injuries from the fall, everyone went to bed. The following morning, once again, there was absolutely no evidence that Greeley had gone down sixteen steps and landed on a cement floor. She was not stiff or sore. She had no bruises or black and blue marks anywhere on her body. The night before we had removed a splinter about the size of a tooth-pick, which was sticking straight out from her elbow. It hadn't even drawn blood.

Since we were scheduled to travel on to Maine that day and she had no apparent problems, we decided to proceed as though nothing had happened.

Greeley never did develop any bruises and she enjoyed a visit with her family as planned.

The only explanation to this remarkable experience was that the Lord Himself or His ministering angels had carried her to the bottom of the steps. When asked recently what she thought about the fall, Greeley smiled and responded: "Why, I think I'm old enough to know better. After all, I was ninety-three at the time!"

(Greeley passed away on January 5, 1996, just three months before her ninety-seventh birthday.)

Angels Delivering

~

Angel in the Passenger Seat
Rod Gammon

URING THE SUMMER between my sophomore and junior years, I was attending summer school classes at Toccoa Falls College and working several jobs to make ends meet.

About two weeks before the incident I am about to relate, I had begun working on the loading docks at United Parcel Service (UPS). It took almost three months to adapt to the physically exhausting work. There were nights when I would collapse on the porch of my aunt and uncle's home, too tired to open the door and crawl into bed.

I will never forget the night an angel joined me on the ride home from work. It was late and deathly dark. I was exhausted, but very excited about my first paycheck and the job that would allow me to get through school.

As I glanced down at the gas gauge, I realized I was driving on fumes and it was twenty miles to the next station! I decided not to turn around to a station I had just passed a few miles back.

As I leaned into a wide bend in the road I hit my high beams. There, in the middle of the road, stood a large dog apparently feeding on roadkill. An image of a small girl weeping for her dead pet flashed in my mind. Killing someone's "Lassie" seemed inevitable.

I jerked the wheel to the right and my world began spinning out of control. Reflexes pulled the wheel hard left to avoid the ditch and "Lassie" too, but the car had its own mind.

As my right tires hit the gravel shoulder it felt as though the car was being pulled into the ditch by an unearthly and powerful force such as I had never before experienced. With all the strength I could muster I pulled the wheel to the left and shot across the south and northbound lanes, bound for the ditch on the other side of the road. With my left wheels heading for a grassy grave, I jerked the wheel right and exploded back onto the pavement. The car began to skid sideways down the road.

I looked over my left shoulder and saw the headlights of an oncoming car. As I braced for the impact, a bright glow suddenly filled the car. I looked to my right. An angel was sitting in the passenger seat! We had no time for deep theological discussions about angels or an immediate future. I just gazed in wonder at his simple but captivating beauty.

Nothing I had ever seen compared to this angel's magnificence. He had medium length, golden-blond wavy hair. His eye were penetrating and brilliantly blue. His face had no blemishes and his skin appeared to suffer no effects of stress or aging. His clothing was all white. I think he even had sandals on his feet, but no wings or halo. His voice was gentle, but strong and very reassuring.

"Don't worry," he said, "we'll be all right."

"Okay," I squeaked as the tires grabbed the road and launched the car into the ditch.

Suddenly, it flipped over. The windshield slammed down over my hands and the steering wheel. With an incredible jolt, the car stopped, the passenger window exploded and I found myself suspended by my seatbelt, hanging upside-down above the crunched roof. I released the belt and crashed headfirst into the shattered glass below.

Something was still wrong though. My right foot was stuck, jammed between the brake and gas pedal. A mental image of a Hollywood-style car explosion flashed in my brain. I knew I had to get out of that pile of mangled metal and glass. I pulled at my foot like an animal caught in a steel trap. It finally released.

The door would not open, so I crawled along the roof of the car and through the window on the passenger side. The tires were still spinning as I stumbled by them through the dust up to the road.

I had no idea what could emerge from this mess. It seemed as though I was at the starting line of a race I did not want to run.

Soon a car pulled up and then another, which went for help. I stumbled around looking for the dog, hoping it had survived. When the police arrived, I told them about the dog and a mailbox I was sure I had hit. Neither could be found. The only damage was the hunk of twisted blue metal, rubber and glass lying in the ditch. I had no cuts or bruises, nor even a slight concussion; only a pulled muscle in my leg from extracting my foot.

An inspection of the car the next day revealed that the roof was crushed all around my head but undamaged where my head would have been. I also noticed that the battery had disconnected itself from anything that could spark gas (or fumes) left in the tank.

I was amazed that I had walked away. From childhood I sensed that God had a special plan for my life. The accident could have ended it before my task was complete, but instead, it became the beginning of an amazing journey of brokenness and dependence on God.

I continue to be assured by the words of God's angelic messenger: "We'll be all right."

Close Call over Ohio
David M. Fields

IT WAS ONE OF THOSE mid-October days when the temperature is still pleasant and the leaves magnificent. Having a custom of exercising my plane at least every other week, I invited my friend Carl and his twelve-year-old grandson to enjoy the colors with me.

The flight was strictly local out of the county airport. After an hour or so in the beautiful fall sky, we decided to head for home. The runway lay east and west and the wind was favorable for a landing toward the east. We entered the landing pattern on the northeastern corner and, according to procedure, announced our intent to the base unit.

I was watching the field to my left as my friend and his grandson peered to the right. Since landing and takeoff are the most dangerous times of a flight, we were on the alert for any traffic nearby. I was especially cautious because there had recently been a couple of near-misses.

But on this Saturday morning nothing was moving and a routine landing was in the offing. Suddenly, the radio came alive as the unmistakable voice of Bill, the airport manager, gave our call number and informed me of a plane off to our right (starboard) side. We looked carefully, but couldn't see anything. I informed Bill that we would keep looking.

Within a few minutes we spotted the plane abeam of us a fair distance away. It was running along the shoreline of the lake to the north, making it difficult to see him. I asked Carl to keep watch and announced over the intercom that I was nearing our turn to the left and south for landing. We had come to the conclusion that the other plane was a flyby, which posed no problem.

After the turn and cutting the power to a quarter, I began to set the Cherokee up for or touchdown. At that point Carl informed me that the other plane was still parallel to us and mimicking our movement, both of us now heading south. I alerted base that Cherokee 667 Fox Trot Lima was turning east for runway nine and added the airport name. There had been no radio transcriptions from the other aircraft.

Just as I lifted the right wing and began to bank the plane to the left, Carl called to me that the other plane was coming straight for us. I applied the throttle and lifted the nose. The mystery plane passed just below us and headed for the runway. Since our elevation at that point was 500 feet, we completed our turn and followed him down. By that time my hair was standing on end.

The landing was picture-perfect and we made the first turnoff for the tie-down area. To our surprise the other craft simply did a touch-and-go to the runway and was off and gone without a word.

As we taxied and did our tie-down we thanked God that Bill had alerted us to the presence of the other plane. Without his help we could have been statistics.

We headed across the blacktop toward the parking area and our vehicle. Just then, Bill appeared in the office door and I headed toward him.

"Thanks, Bill, for being so observant. We did not see that plane."

Bill look puzzled.

"I don't know what you're talking about, Dave. I never called you on the radio and I haven't been out of the office until just now. With no windows on the north side of the building I couldn't have possibly seen any traffic in that direction. In fact, no one has used the radio for some time. We heard you call us but had no idea what you were talking about."

Who, then, had warned us of the other plane? Whose voice was it that sounded just like Bill's?

Nobody spoke until we were in the car. But once we realized what had happened and how grateful we should be to be alive, we bubbled over with praise to the Lord for His goodness. Apparently God knew about three of His children flying around the beautiful autumn sky and had sent His angel to bring them safely back to earth.

The Man in the Old White Car
Edward Nanno

WHAT HAPPENED TO ME is my story. I cannot prove that I was visited by an angel. I only know that this uncommon encounter happened in my life at a point of desperation and it became the catalyst that caused me to become a believer in Jesus Christ.

I was the oldest of eight children from a divorced family not willing to deal with its alcohol abuse. Consequently, I began drinking at an early age and by eighteen was myself an alcoholic.

Although I continued drinking, I was able to work steadily. I married, had two children and a home life, which I considered to be quite normal.

When the Vietnam war ended, I found a new way to lift my spirits— marijuana. I was soon spending a quarter of my weekly income on the new habit and began to realize that selling it to others would take care of this vice in a way that was profitable as well as personally satisfying. I sold only to adults, thereby releasing any guilt associated with this new business venture.

At the time, I was working with a bricklayer named Carmen. He claimed to be a born-again Christian, but I saw nothing in his life that seemed any better than my own. However, when I ran into him on a job a few years later, he was different, a man who practiced what he preached.

He told me about sin. I already knew I was a sinner. He told me the penalty of sin was death, but that Jesus died in my place and if I put my trust in Him I

174

could avoid this penalty. I understood what he was saying, but at age twenty-six I was having the time of my life, drinking, gambling, hanging out at strip joints and partying my paycheck away. Religion was something that could wait.

Carmen continued living his Christianity in front of me, doing the hard jobs himself, working outside in the cold while I worked inside, taking me home for lunch a couple times a week. When I commented on his goodness, he would tell me it wasn't him, it was Jesus. Time would reveal that his faithful witness was backed up by faithful prayer.

In 1978 we moved to Florida. It was there that I became dependent on cocaine. Cocaine was very different from alochol and marijuana and I soon found myself a total slave to it. Because it was expensive (using up $500 more per week than I made), I realized that selling it was my only hope of maintaining my own habit.

It was during this emotional upheaval that I began to read the Bible Carmen had given me. The struggle, I know now, was actually a spiritual one. Satan was determined to keep me.

On a Sunday night in February 1981 I was working on my friend Tom's fireplace. Tom was my connection to everything abusive money could buy. Our various dependencies made us fast friends and eventually business partners, selling cocaine to others. I was finished for the day, waiting for Tom to come back with more beer and more cocaine.

Anxious to get home, I decided to just go ahead and take his car and head onto I-95 toward Pompano Beach. I noticed a van starting to pass me. Thinking someone was out to kill me, I swerved, lost control and headed for a bridge abutment. In the middle of the skid, I cried, "Jesus, if You exist, help me out of this and I will change my life."

Still doing at least sixty miles per hour, I struck the abutment, bounced back onto the highway, across two lanes of traffic and stopped. Cut and bleeding and with two previous DUI convictions, I decided to leave the wrecked car and get as far away as possible. But there was nowhere to go. My only choice was to walk down the shoulder of the highway.

I had not gone far when a beat-up white car pulled next to me and stopped.

"Do you need help?" the driver asked. "Jesus told me to pick you up."

"Boy, do I need help," I answered. "I've had an accident and I've got to get home before I'm picked up by the police."

"Well, get in," he said. "The Lord Told me to take you wherever you want to go."

My rescuer was a black man with a Caribbean accent. A load of boxes filled the backseat of his car and a white cross hung from his rearview mirror.

"Why did you stop?" I asked as I climbed in. "I wasn't hitchhiking."

"I told you, I was driving down the highway and Jesus told me to stop and pick you up."

"You have got to be kidding," I replied. "I just prayed a prayer like that."

"Well, then, your prayer is answered. Where do you want to go?"

As we drove toward my house, he told me how much Jesus loved me and asked me if I knew that Jesus died for my sins. I told him that Carmen had already said the same things.

As we pulled into my driveway, I thanked him and tried to hand him a $50 bill. He told me he didn't need my money.

"Just thank Jesus," he said.

"I do thank Jesus and I thank you too. How about giving the money to your church?" I suggested.

"I don't have a church," he replied. When I saw there was no more arguing with him, I got out of the car. He told me once again to thank Jesus and I turned toward the house.

Drunk, cut and bleeding, I knocked on the door and my wife let me in. I told her I'd had an accident and that this guy (pointing down the street) had given me a ride home. But there was no car to be seen.

The next day we went to the police station and I turned myself in. Miraculously, they didn't arrest me. My prayer that night wasn't just to get me out of a mess. I had done business with God and my life began to change. When I called out to Jesus for help, He sent an old white car with a Caribbean driver. I believe he was an angel.

Angels and Prayer

Special Delivery

Lois Dungan

Y HUSBAND AND I were missionaries to the deaf in Jamaica for seventeen years. Prior to our going, we were to raise our own support in the amount of $500 per month. We had managed to acquire only $335 but the Mission still begged us to come. So, we went, believing that the Lord would help make up the difference...somehow.

Over the following years, support would often be lacking. On one occasion, our income dropped to only $150. My husband and I wondered if we should talk it over with the Mission board or just leave it in the Lord's hands. We decided on the latter.

About two months later, on the very day the board arrived for their annual meeting, I went to the post office to pick up our mail. To our surprise, one of the letters contained $475 from a person we did not know. We phoned our family in the U.S. to see if they knew this person. They did not. We sent a thank-you letter, a receipt and a promise to visit the lady when we returned for a break.

That July, while we were home, we met out benefactor. She told us the following story.

She owned a small ceramics business and had promised the Lord she would give half of her net earnings to missions. Her profit for the year had amounted to $950. When she asked the Lord to tell her where to send the money, our faces came to her mind. She had heard us speak at a church but had no idea of our address. So she told the Lord (and no one else), "If you want me to send the money to the Dungans, you will have to get me the address."

The next morning when she opened the front door, our prayer card—complete with address—was lying on her front steps. She was never able to find out who put it there.

As far as we're concerned, we believe an angel left it there in response to our prayer.

Guards in White!

Alice G. Young

THE LITTLE PHILIPPINE VILLAGE of Bayanan lay silent in the summer night. Alone on a mat in her palm-thatched, wall-less home, missionary Hazel Page watched the trees sway in the gentle breeze.

Usually the villagers sent one or two of their children to stay with her. But tonight the men of the village were not yet back from doing some work for the lowlanders, so the women kept their children with them. As was her habit, Hazel committed herself to God and, assured of His protection, fell asleep.

Thousands of miles away in British Columbia, Canada, Hazel's mother suddenly awoke, fear stabbing at her heart. Her daughter was in danger! She knelt beside her bed and prayed that God would care for her and meet her need, whatever it might be.

Hazel was awakened by loud voices wafting in the open windows. The men of the village had returned. Hazel knew by the sound of their voices that several of them were drunk.

"Let's kill her," one voice louder than the others shouted. "We'll see if there is a God. I don't believe there is a God. Let's kill her!"

Hazel sat up on her sleeping mat trying to get a glimpse of the main trail into the village. In her heart she knew she was the one they were intending to kill. She also knew that there was no way to protect herself, no way to escape.

"Dear Lord," she prayed, "You are able to save me. Help me now. But whatever happens, may Your will be done!"

The fear left her and she waited quietly in the darkness, listening for approaching footsteps. She could see no one but she could hear the rowdy voices coming closer. As they reached the path that led to Hazel's little house, suddenly there was silence—several minutes of silences—followed by subdued talking far away in the village.

"Thank You, Lord," Hazel prayed, "thank You for saving me." She was sure the Lord had delivered her, but how she did not know.

The next morning, as usual, many visitors came to her house. The villagers loved to talk and watch her work. Some of them came for medicine or to have their cuts treated.

"Were you afraid last night?" one finally asked. "The men came home drunk after working on the road and they were going to kill you."

"Well," responded Hazel, "I was afraid at first. I wondered what was going to happen. But I prayed to my Heavenly Father to look after me and I was not afraid then."

"It was David," the visitor added. "He came home from town drunk as he often does. The others said that he was the one who shouted, 'Let's kill her.' They all started along the trail, but when they reached the path to your hut, David suddenly stopped in his tracks. The others wanted to know what was wrong. Instead of answering, David led them into the village."

"Guards! There were guards dressed in white standing in the path," David finally told the men. "I was afraid to try to pass them."

Sometime later, David himself came to Hazel. "What would have happened to me if I had tried to kill a servant of such a great God?" he asked her.

Hazel told the frightened man that God is a merciful God who forgives sin and takes away guilt, and would become his Savior if he asked Him. Right there, David prayed to receive forgiveness through Jesus Christ.

In the next mail from Canada, Hazel received a letter from her mother.

"I had a phone call from Mrs. Young this morning," it said. "She woke up early feeling that she ought to pray for you, that you needed special prayer. I am sure this was no accident, because I was awake at the same time and I too felt that I should pray for you. That would have been early evening in the Philippines. Did anything happened?"

Most certainly something happened! God sent His protecting angels in answer to prayer.

Reprinted with permission from *Pioneer Girls Trails Magazine*, January 1964 issue.

Denny

Deborah Menzies

WE HAD GOTTEN AWAY far too late that day. But moving is hard, especially when having to say good-bye to friends and parents.

My husband Dale, accompanied by our two-year-old daughter, was driving the largest moving van we could rent. I followed in our small but fully packed car. Our then four-month-old daughter and the dog would keep me company on the long trip north.

The traffic through Los Angeles was painfully slow and about two hours later we finally stopped at Culver City for Dale to run an errand. While he was gone, I gave the children a break from their car seats and, putting my purse on the sidekick of the van, proceeded to play our favorite game of chase.

When Dale returned, we agreed to backtrack about a mile to a burger restaurant, eat supper and then drive until we could go no farther.

We were almost at the restaurant before I remembered that I had left my purse on the sidekick. My heart stopped. The purse contained not only the usual driver's license and credit cards, but also the down payment on our future home and all the identification necessary to get our family moved across the Canadian border. I knew that it could take weeks, maybe even months, to replace them.

Dale had not even parked the van when I ran from the car shouting. "My purse! My purse! do you have my purse?"

"I never saw your purse," he replied, looking very confused.

As I ran back to the car, I gave him the quick version of what had happened and then drove back to the place where the whole incident started. My purse was not there!

Oblivious to the impatient and boisterous drivers following me, I slowly retraced every foot of the mile-long trek. My heart was pounding. My head was racing. *How could I have done this?* I scolded myself. *Lord, I need you. Please find my purse. Send someone to help. I need a miracle. Oh, show me what to do!*

Dale was getting something to eat for Breanna when I walked into the restaurant.

"Did you find it?" he asked anxiously.

"No! Maybe you should take a look," was my disappointed reply. He gave me some money and told me to eat something while I waited for him to return.

I could not eat. All I could do was pray for a miracle. I gave each thought, each question and each doubt to God and felt confident, in an anxious sort of way, that God would give us guidance as to what to do next.

Dale came back empty-handed and proceeded to start the phone calls necessary to cancel credit cards and get the ball rolling toward reordering the most urgent paperwork.

"Wait a minute!" I interrupted, "Before you cancel anything, we should call Mom and Dad's house. I know its a long shot, but if someone honest found my purse, they may be trying to get ahold of me."

My sister Jackie answered. I barely had time to say "hello," when she interrupted me.

"Debbie, I've been so worried. This man named Denny called," she said. "He has your purse! What happened?"

I gave her a brief rundown of the events of the past few hours and told her I would explain further after I took care of the business at hand.

Denny had given Jackie two phone numbers. I assumed one was his home number and one his work number. I quickly dialed the first and was greeted with a cheery hello. He knew immediately who I was. I thanked him for contacting me and asked if I could come and pick up the purse.

"That's all right," he replied, "I'll come to you." After trying to convince him otherwise, I gave him the name of the restaurant and returned to the table to wait.

Within minutes, I looked to see a young man clutching my purse . He was average in height, fairly thin, and was wearing a T-shirt and blue jeans with holes in the knees. His mousy brown hair was long and scraggly. I remembered thinking to myself that this man did not fit my image of an honest person.

We shook hands and I thanked him over and over for his honesty and help. When he handed me the purse, I instinctively started opening the zipper to check the contents.

"Don't worry, Debbie, it's all there," he said.

I could feel the heat rising in my cheeks. I felt foolish for doubting his honesty. We talked for a few minutes, then I thanked him once more and he left.

I ran to the phone to report back to Jackie. We agreed that I should do something for Denny, so I asked her to call him back to get his address. The least I could do was to mail him a thank-you note.

Later that evening Jackie called the first number and was greeted by a recording stating that the number had been disconnected! She tried again. Disconnected! She dialed the second number. The person who answered said she must have the wrong number because there was no Denny there, nor had there ever been a Denny there!

The following evening I called to get Denny's address. When Jackie told me he could not be found, I was puzzled.

"Are you sure you dialed the correct number? And you asked for Denny? How could he be there one hour and not the next? He couldn't have just disappeared. I shook hands with him!

"I think he was your guardian angel!" It was mother's voice as she came on the line. A tingling sensation went through my body. Up until that moment I knew God had answered our prayers, but I assumed He had just prompted a young man to carry out the job. It had not occurred to me that Denny could be an angel.

Then, as if my eyes were opened, I knew who he really was. I had prayed that God would send "someone" to help and He chose to send an angel!

During the four-day journey to Canada, we encountered one difficulty after another. God provided all the miracles we needed, but I will always remember this miracle as the most special of all—the day I met an angel named Denny.

Lord, Help Me!
Miriam Charter

I ALWAYS FEEL A BIT HESITANT to speak about my encounters with angels. Skeptics may tell me I was hallucinating, that I was lucky or that my experiences were just coincidences.

But the Bible says there are angels, and I have sensed their presence in my life on special occasions. My prayer is that, in sharing my story, you will be reassured of the ministry of His angels on your behalf, and that you will go into each day with a new awareness of God's constant watchcare over you. Truly, "he will command his angels concerning you to guard you in all your ways" (Psalm 91:11).

Leaning hard into the icy wind of the early morning, I mounted the steps to the train station, my two bags dead weights in my hands. I was traveling alone, not an enviable position for anyone in an unfamiliar country in Eastern Europe.

It was 6 A.M. and already the station was crowded with people—peasants with their wooden farm tools, gypsies huddled together to keep warm, military men in faded uniforms, sad-faced men and women—all bent on going somewhere on this early winter day.

It had been a tension-filled and lonely journey for me, and I was ready to go home. The prospect of this train ride to Bucharest and then a flight from there to Western Europe was not a comforting one. The connections in the capital were tight, but not impossible.

I checked the crude departure board to verify the time of my train's arrival in the station—6:25 on platform two with only a two-minute stop before departure. The icy wind convinced me to wait inside the smoke-filled waiting room rather than out on the platform. I would need only to cross the track of line one to board my train.

At 6:23 I heard the muffled announcement of the arrival of the train going to the capital. It was on track two. But as I gathered my bags, another train, loaded with passengers, pulled into the station on track one. The entrance to every car was packed with peasants and gypsies with pigs, chickens and stacks of dirty bundles—all in transit somewhere.

Instantly, I realized my predicament. The train on line one was blocking my access to the train on line two. I could never walk around it in two minutes, nor could I imagine hoisting myself and my two bags onto this crowded train and pushing my way through the animals, people and bundles to try to exit on the other side. I was afraid of getting caught in the press of the first train and being transported away to some unknown destination.

My train was pulling in on track two for its two-minute stop. Time was short. The seconds seemed like hours as I saw the impossibility of the situation.

"Lord, help me!" was all I could cry.

Instantly, a man was at my side, taking the two bags from my hands. He said only two words (whether in English or his own language, I do not recall). I only know I understood him to be saying, "Follow me!"

As he climbed into the humanity-packed train on line one, the crowd in the entrance fell back. I followed. Like the waters of the Red Sea, the crowd parted as we climbed through the car and descended onto platform two. He handed me my bags. I turned to thank him, but he had disappeared! The train was already moving out of the station as I climbed aboard.

I sank to a seat, my mind turning to my deliverer. Who was this helpful man who, without a word, had seen and understood my predicament? Where had he come from and why had he disappeared? As the train sped toward the capital and my subsequent flight to Vienna, I felt strangely comforted and surrounded by a wonderful Presence.

Adapted by permission from *Alliance Life*, September 26, 1990.

Angels and the Dying

The Homegoing
Joan Ruth Hand

I T HAPPENED in the very early hours of June 11, 1946. I will never forget the date because it was the day the Lord chose to take my mother home.

Sound asleep in my upstairs bedroom, I awoke suddenly to see a light outlining the east window on the wall opposite my bed. Instantly I knew my mother had died. Her death was not unexpected. She had been in failing health for a number of years.

Then, unexpectedly, I felt the gentle pressure of a hand closing my eyelids and an inaudible message being relayed to my spirit: "Don't be afraid, child," the messenger said, "your mother has just gone home to be with her precious Lord. She is at peace now and all is well with her soul. You may now go back to sleep."

How could a teenager go back to sleep after she's been told her mother is dead? But that is exactly what happened. I settled down to a sound and peaceful sleep without even shedding a tear. That was a miracle in itself as I am an emotional person and cry very easily.

When my dad woke me the next morning, he did not have to tell me the news. I made it easy for him by telling him I already knew that Mother was gone. What a gracious daddy to allow his daughter to sleep through (or so he thought!) rather than to break the disturbing news in the middle of the night. And what a loving and caring Heavenly Father to send His comforting messenger to me to console and reassure a teenage girl. I have always felt it was truly my guardian angel reporting for duty!

Songs for a Heaven-Sent Boy

Marjorie Ann Lumley

ABOUT 9:30 P.M. ON SEPTEMBER 26, 1967, my three-year-old Frederick cried out in his sleep. Frightened by the intensity of his cry, his seven-year-old sister Jennifer came running to the kitchen where I was working.

I ran to the bedroom and asked Frederick what was wrong. He said he didn't know, but he didn't feel well. I asked him if he wanted me to rock him. He nodded. I carried him into the dining room and we sat together in the painted blue rocker.

"Does anything hurt you?" I asked gently.

"I don't know, Mommy," he responded, his eyes focusing on mine. Then, searchingly, he asked, "Are I going to die?"

"No!" I answered firmly.

Frederick settled into my arms and fell asleep as we rocked together. About 11 o'clock I carried him back to bed and went to my own room unaware of just how sick my little boy really was.

As I lay in the darkness rehearsing the events of the preceding hour or so, I heard what sounded like a radio playing in the distance. The music came closer and closer and I became aware that my whole house was filled with the most beautiful singing voices I had ever heard. It seemed like the sound of a thousand angels singing with great joy. Pure delight! I was unable to wake my husband Fred and I lay there in wonder trying to understand what the angels were singing.

Although I could not understand even one word, I breathed in the beauty and didn't question why this was happening. Tremendous exaltation, love, sweetness and vitality flowed up and down, surrounding our home in the ongoing crescendos.

Too soon the voices began to fade and finally, silence. The next morning I had no recollection of the heavenly choir.

Frederick was playing in his bedroom when I got up. He had emptied his entire toy closet onto the floor. And there, standing taller than I believed possible in the midst of it all, were two towers of blocks, solid and stable. I sat down with him and played awhile.

Back in the kitchen, I assumed Frederick was still playing in his bedroom. But when I went to check on him, he was not there. I found him curled up sleeping on the couch in the dining room.

I touched his forehead. It was hot.

"I so sick," he said when I roused him. I took his temperature. It was very high. Unable to drive because of foot surgery the previous day, I called the doctor. He promised to come by after office hours.

I bathed Frederick with cool cloths and watched his temperature rise. By the time the doctor arrived, Frederick was in a coma. On his cheek lay one little tear. His brother Richard and sister Jennifer arrived on the school bus just in time to look in the ambulance. The love that Frederick—a tiny, heaven-sent angel—and I shared enveloped me as he was rushed to the hospital.

His death from meningitis came so swiftly. As his father and I sat contemplating the events of the previous twenty-four hours, I suddenly remembered the angel choir. Even though I didn't know God at the time, God knew me. I believe He sent those angels to speak love and assurance to me during one of the most difficult experiences of my life—and to welcome Frederick joyfully into God's kingdom.

Twenty-seven years later, I heard them again. For years I had cried behind closed doors that no one loved me. I now believe that God saw my need and sent his special messengers to minister His love to me in full measure. For three years and four months I was blessed by the total and innocent love in the eyes and actions of my darling Frederick, and the love of God for me in the songs of the angels. To know that God loves and cares for me is heaven on earth.

You will now understand by Frederick's headstone reads: May God's angels always sing for Frederick Lumley Chapman, May 18, 1964—September 27, 1967.

~ *Endnotes* ~

Chapter One

1. Stephen W. Hawking, *A Brief History of Time* (New York: Bantam trade paper edition, June 1990), p. 11.
2. This is the contention of Nelson Pacheco and Tommy Blann in *Unmasking the Enemy* (Arlington, VA: Bendan Press). "We are dealing with highly intelligent beings," says Pacheco, "and in their effort to subvert us, they will use whatever cover they can." It wouldn't be the first time. In Galatians 1:8, the apostle Paul envisages a false messenger appearing as an angel from heaven to proclaim false hope to a confused and fickle generation.
3. John G. Paton, *Missionary to the New Hebrides: An Autobiography.* First Part (New York: Fleming H. Revell Company, 1889).
4. Cecil Wightwick Haywood, *How God Won the War—1918—The White Cavalry* (Vancouver, B.C.: British Israel Prayer League), pp. 19-20.
5. Sophie Burnham, *A Book of Angels* (New York: Ballantine Books, 1990), pp. 21-22.
6. Marilyn Carlson Webber and William D. Webber, *A Rustle of Angels* (Carmel: Guide Posts, 1994), p. 10.
7. John MacArthur, *God, Satan, and Angels* (Chicago: Moody Press, 1989), p. 132.

Chapter Two

1. Billy Graham, *Angels: God's Secret Agents* (Waco, TX: Word Books, 1986), p. 45.
2. Jim Dethmer, "Three Things God Loves: Laughter" (Chicago: Seeds Tape Ministry, Willow Creek Community Church), AM9031.

Chapter Three

1. Billy Graham, *Angels: God's Secret Agents* (Waco, TX: Word Books, 1986), p. 17.

Chapter Four

1. John MacArthur, Jr., *God, Satan and Angels*, (Chicago: Moody Press, 1989), pp. 171–172

2. John Bunyan, *Pilgrim's Progress in Today's English* (Chicago: The Moody Bible Institute of Chicago, 1964), p. 191.

Chapter Five

1. Donna Hinkle Lagerquist, "Nothing to It," Copyright 1992 by Willow Creek Community Church. Used by permission of Zondervan Publishing House.

2. C.S. Lewis, *The Screwtape Letters* (Toronto: S.J. Reginald Saunders Publisher, 1945), p. 40.

3. John MacArthur, Jr., *God, Satan and Angels* (Chicago: Moody Press, 1989) p. 69.

4. C.S. Lewis, p. 39.

5. *Might Magazine* July/August, 1996, #12, p. 41.

6. Ibid., p. 43.

7. Ibid., p. 47.

8. Donald Grey Barnhouse, *The Invisible War* (Grand Rapids, MI: Zondervan Publishing House, 1965), p. 59.

9. John MacArthur, Jr., p. 80.

Chapter Six

1. C.S. Lewis, as quoted by Scott Peck in *People of the Lie* (New York: Simon and Schuster, 1983), p. 83.

2. Donald Grey Barnhouse, *The Invisible War* (Grand Rapids, MI: Zondervan Publishing House, 1965), p. 169.

3. Ibid.

4. John Milton, *Paradise Lost:* Book X: The Norton Anthology of English Lieterature, Third Edition (New York: W. W. Norton and Company, 1962), pp. 782–783.

Chapter Seven

1. Texe Marrs, *Dark Secrets of the New Age* (Westchester, IL: Crossway Books, 1987), pp. 95–96.

2. Ibid., p. 97.

3. Ibid., pp. 95, 96.

4. *New Age Journal,* April 30, 1995, p. 31.

5. Pat Rodegast and Judith Stanton, compilers, *Emmanuel's Book: A Manual for Living Comfortably in the Cosmos* (New York: Bantam Books, 1985), p. 84.

6. J.Z. Knight. *Ramtha: Voyage to the New World* (New York: Ballantine, 1987), p. 219, as cited by John Ankerberg and John Weldon in *The Facts on Spirit Guides: How to Avoid the Seduction of the Spirit World and Demonic Powers* (Eugene, OR: Harvest House Publishers, 1988), p. 21.

7. T.S. Eliot, "Choruses from 'The Rock.'" *T.S. Eliot: Collected Poems 1909–1962* (London: Faber and Faber, 1963), p. 170.

8. J.Z. Knight, pp. 61, 136, respectively.

9. Helen Schucman, *A Course on Miracles, Combined Volume, Second Edition, Workbook for Students* (New York: The Penguin Group, 1996), Part I: 342, 363.

10. Rodegast and Stanton, p. 44.

11. Alma Daniel, Timothy Wyllie, Andrew Ramer, *Ask Your Angels* (New York: Ballantine, 1992).

12. "The New Spirituality," *Maclean's Magazine* . October 10, 1994, p. 47.

13. *Rolling Stone*, Issue 740, August 8, 1996, pp. 20–21.
14. Rodegast and Stanton, pp. 61, 78.
15. Ibid., p. 201.
16. Ibid., p. 205.
17. Ibid., p. 228.
18. James Houston, *In Search of Happiness* (Oxford: A Lion Book, 1990), p. 130.
19. Rodegast and Stanton, p. 29.
20. Helen Schucman, Part I: 168.
21. Daniel, Wyllie and Ramer, p. 56.
22. *TIME* , December 27, 1993, "Angels Among Us," p. 46.
23. Rodegast and Stanton, pp. 76, 77.
24. Daniel, Wyllie and Ramer, p. 57.
25. Rodegast and Stanton, p. 61.
26. John Oxenham, "The Ways," *Poems That Live Forever* (New York: Doubleday, 1965), p. 300.

Chapter Eight

1. Gail Harvey, *On the Wings of Angels* (New York: Gramercy Books, 1993), p. 5.

Chapter Nine

1. Mother Teresa, as cited by Lee Strobel, *What Jesus Would Say?* (Grand Rapids, MI: Zondervan Publishing House, 1994), pp. 70–71.

Chapter 10

1. Mark Twain, *Report from Paradise* (New York: Harper and Brothers Publishers, 1952), p. 38.
2 Ibid., xviii. "Neither Howells [Clemens' friend] nor I believe in hell or the

divinity of the Savior, but no matter, the Savior is none the less a sacred Personage, and a man should have no desire or disposition to refer to him lightly, profanely, or otherwise than with the profoundest reverence."